M.S.PLATT   THE LAST SUPPER

THE LAST SUPPER
(The Second Coming of Jesus
Christ in Our Time)

M.S. PLATT

Copyright © 2016 by M.S. Platt
ISBN: 978-0-9966845-3-8

All rights reserved. No part of this book may be reproduced or transmitted in any form or by any means, electronic or mechanical, including photocopying, recording, or by any information storage and retrieval system, without permission from the copyright owner.

This is a work of fiction. Names, characters, places and incidents either are the product of the author's imagination or are used fictitiously, and any resemblance to any actual persons, living or dead, events, or locals is entirely coincidental.

M.S.PLATT   THE LAST SUPPER

This book was printed in the United States of America.
To order additional copies of this book, contact:
Amazon.com

>Dedicated to:
>
>Linda Higbie
>
>Sandra Chaff

M.S.PLATT   THE LAST SUPPER

Table of Contents

Chapter I	Page	5
Chapter II	Page	18
Chapter III	Page	30
Chapter IV	Page	48
Chapter V	Page	83
Chapter VI	Page	116
Chapter VII	Page	129
Chapter VIII	Page	141
Chapter IX	Page	151
Chapter X	Page	164
Chapter XI	Page	175
Chapter XII	Page	191
Chapter XIII	Page	213
Chapter XIV	Page	223
Map of the Middle East	Page	227
Attributions	Page	228

M.S.PLATT   THE LAST SUPPER

Forward

Why read a story about a conflict between the Middle East and the powers of the West? The answer is simple. That conflict has been going on for 1400 years and may culminate in a nuclear holocaust and the end of civilization, as we know it. The author suggests that this catastrophe can be averted if the Messiah, Jesus Christ, returns to earth and prevents it. How is that possible?

During the course of this novel, the author portrays a convoluted tale of mystery and intrigue, and of history, politics and philosophy leading up to the Second Coming of Jesus and explains why the world now needs to seek brotherly love as taught by Jesus.

M.S.PLATT   THE LAST SUPPER

CHAPTER I

In Israel, when the barley crop has matured and fully harvested, when the snows of Mount Hermon have begun to melt, and the winds of winter have mellowed, Jews turn to a new season and welcome the Feast of Matzos, their Passover, for as it is said in Exodus 12:14:

"This day shall become a remembrance to you and you shall celebrate it as a festival for the LORD; for your generations as an eternal decree."

It is in recognition that the Israelites, the Hebrews, gained their freedom from slavery—from Pharaoh -- from Egypt—that this day is celebrated. And friends and family gather from far and wide to meet, and share this historic event.

M.S.PLATT   THE LAST SUPPER

So it was that I, David ben Moshe, my Jewish name, David Adams, my American name, now Professor of History at Boston University had arranged to spend the holiday. I had invited a dear friend, and old classmate, Neville Hudson from London, to join me, and the two of us would go to Israel, to Tel Aviv and beyond, and share old memories of our past, and to meet new friends and new experiences.

The flight from Logan was uneventful—almost boring. It started late on the previous evening, and now, as the sun's golden halo broke over the mist and clouds over Heathrow, I looked forward to seeing Neville again. Neville, archeologist and explorer, had just spent six months in Mesopotamia and Iran, and we were going to spend the first meal of the Passover, the Seder, together with my family in Tel Aviv. Neville had just explored some caves in southwestern Iran/Persia near Shushan, now called Shush, and had written to me that he had some amazing findings to share. He hinted that it might shed some light on the mystery of the long lost ten tribes of Israel, allegedly lost some twenty-six hundred years ago.

M.S.PLATT   THE LAST SUPPER

We had been undergraduate buddies at Harvard, each from different parts of the world. I was from the midwest, he from Edinburgh, Scotland. The four years that we spent together in college served as a matrix for our ensuing relationship-- through the years of training during our graduate and postgraduate studies, through the joys of sharing insightful concepts and light moments of laughter, through reams of paper correspondence and short transatlantic telephone calls. But we never forgot the true essence of life as quoted by Socrates: "A life not fully examined, is a life not worth living."

Fortunately the flight had arrived on time and after a short jaunt to the baggage claim area, I began to look for Neville.

"Are you lost old chap?'

I turned, and there was Neville looking at me --ever confident. His face had not changed much. It was the same classical, angular Brit face and muscular body; but now, his grey hair was quite short, and he was laughing at me like a mischievous schoolboy.

M.S.PLATT   THE LAST SUPPER

"Neville, you old dog", I replied. "It's wonderful seeing you again. You still look damn good. I assume you have that great tan from working in the fields?"

"And you, David", he chuckled, "haven't gone to pot either. I wondered all night waiting for you at the airport what you would look like. You are better looking that the photos that you have sent me over the years."

"Thank you, old friend, for the compliment, but I am famished! Is there a café in this airport where we can get some coffee?"

"Yes. Right down the hallway, but we must hurry. We need to check our luggage at the British Airways counter to get our flight to Ben-Gurion. We only have a few hours before departure."

"Neville, you're right. Let's hurry."

As Neville led the way he turned to smile at me. "And I will entrance you with stories of my travels in Iran."

We picked up our luggage and registered them at the ticket counter and hurriedly moved to the café. It was empty because of the early hour, and we got served quickly. As we sat down, Neville observed me again and said, "You haven't gained a bloody ounce since we were undergraduates, David. Still weigh about 130 pounds, I gather?"

"Right on the button. How do you do it?"

"Years of training. I pick up a bone and guess the height and weight of its owner. Neat trick, eh?"

"I am impressed! And how is your wife, Kristin? Is she coming along?"

"No. She has to finish some lectures at the University. I hope that she will join us next week during the Easter break. And I trust that you still have not married. What are you waiting for? You know that we men need companionship as we age. Or are you too busy in your work to miss the friendship and stimulation of home life?"

"Yeah, and the conflict of home life. No I can wait for that. So tell me. What is this big mystery that you want to share with me? And how did you ever get to western Iran in the first place?"

Neville's face brightened. "Well, the Iranians wanted to show good faith following the nuclear deals so they allowed a few archeologists to explore their country's historical sites. Not their "peaceful" nuclear research areas, mind you, but for archeological reasons, elsewhere in the country. That is why I got to go to Shushan in the southwestern edge of the country near the Zagros Mountains that separate Iraq from the old Persian/Medes areas. I had a hunch that some biblical resources might be found there. I knew that Henry Rawlinson and A.H. Layard had explored Iranian sites in 1836 and that William Loftus identified Susa, the site of Shushan in 1851. A number of French explorers conducted major excavations from the turn of the century to the beginning of World War I. They even identified the palaces of Darius and Xerxes. There was an interlude after the first war, but after World War II, some work was undertaken. Roman Ghirshman took over in 1946, and he continued until the late 1960's. In fact, Jean Perrot and his group identified the sites described in the Book of Esther. The Iranian revolution in 1979 put a stop to all of that. Then came the fresh air of entente, and I had my chance. I postulated that the Assyrians deported the northern Hebrew Israelites from Samaria to Persia as well as Babylonia in 720 BCE. And that would lead me to some clues.

" And, David, to learn what happened to the ten tribes, you need to know some of the history of that era.

"Yeah. I know," I interrupted. "But as far as I am concerned it all relates to the catastrophic reigns of the Israelite kings after King David. The ancient Israelites never paid attention to the words of their Torah. In Deuteronomy 17, they were admonished that no king "shall have many wives nor amass silver and gold to excess." And the prophet Samuel warned them that a king would take a tenth of their property and make the people his slaves. These events actually came true. King Solomon forced his people to go to Lebanon and work as laborers while he built the First Temple, and he had a harem of 700 wives and 300 concubines! Well, what happened when King Solomon died? The kingdom split into a northern Samaria and southern Judah. Judah worshipped the God of Moses, Yahweh. That word was never translated but addressed as HASHEM, THE NAME, The Name of the LORD. The northern kingdom worshipped both Yahweh and Baal, the idol of the Canaanites. This breach of faith was contrary to the Torah, the law given to Moses by their God. Turbulence quickly ensued in the land for the next 200-300 years. Recurrent assassinations occurred in over half of the kingships. Of note is the fact that their Ten

M.S.PLATT   THE LAST SUPPER

Commandments prohibited murder. In fact, Samaria and Judah frequently warred with each other. In 732 BCE, the Samarians threatened the southern kingdom in Jerusalem. King Ahab, the king of Judah, paid tribute to Tiglath-Pilester of Assyria for protection. That debt continued, but Babylonia eventually conquered Judah in 586 BCE. In the meantime, Shalmaneser V of Assyria besieged Samaria in 732 BCE and Sargon, his successor, captured the nation in 720 BCE. Sargon allegedly exiled the ten tribes to Assyria.

   Neville smiled at me. "Well done, David. But there is more to the story. In the second decade of the sixth century, the Assyrian Empire crumbled due to recurrent civil war. By 612 BCE, the Medes of Persia and the Babylonians captured Ninevah, the capital of Assyria. The Neo-Assyrian Empire collapsed by 605 BCE. Meanwhile, the Babylonian Empire gained strength, and under King Nebuchadnezzar conquered Jerusalem and Judah in 586 BCE. The nobility of Judah was exiled to Babylon, and in accord with my research, some to Persia.

   Neville continued. "Some of the Jews became advisors to the Babylonian kings. Daniel was one of them. He warned Belshazzar, the grandson of Nebuchadnezzar, that the Persians would conquer Babylonia. It appears that the rise in power by some of the Jews became a threat to the established Babylonian hierarchy. Even Daniel was sent to a lion's den. Look at the Daniel stories in the Old Testament for that history.

"And that was not all," Neville added. "The wars in Mesopotamia and Persia continued. Cyrus joined with the Persians and overthrew Astyages, the king of the Medes in 550 BCE. Thus started the Persian Empire. Did the Jews in Persia help in this venture? I wonder. Look at the history. In 539 BCE, Cyrus issued a proclamation allowing all the expelled peoples in Persia, including the Jews, to return to their homelands. One copy of that decree is on the Cyrus Cylinder that is now in our British Museum. Did the Jews help Cyrus in the venture to overtake the Medes? I wonder. Why did Cyrus even give the Jews permission to rebuild the Temple? The Old Testament prophets Ezra and Nehemiah did document that event, but the Samarians who had remained in the northern kingdom rebelled, and the project was delayed. Construction re-ensued when Darius I who reigned from 522 to 486 BCE later gave permission, and the Second Temple was completed about 516 BCE. Darius even allegedly donated wood for the construction! His son, Xerxes I, also known as Ahasuerus in the Book of Esther, reigned from 486 to 465 BCE."

"What do you think happened to the Jews who remained in Babylonia and Persia?" I asked.

"David, it is conceivable that the nobles from the northern kingdom who worshipped Baal assimilated with the Assyrians, and later, the Babylonian cultures. Those that still worshipped Yahweh seemed to resist assimilation. These Jews also became active in Babylonian and Persian culture. They became influential and wealthy citizens. Daniel was one of them.

"Sounds familiar, doesn't it, David. The same story took place in the Book of Esther when Haman, representing the Persian establishment during Esther's time, wanted to kill all the Jews in Persia."

I shrugged my shoulders and fronded. "That's a recurrent theme in Jewish history, Neville. The Jews become a vital part of a culture and when they attain too much power or wealth, the establishment turns against them. Think of the expulsion of the Jews from

M.S.PLATT   THE LAST SUPPER

England by King Edward I in 1290 CE. Think of the anti-Semitism of the late 19th Century and the destruction of eastern European Jewry by Hitler and the Nazis. Are these not replays of a similar theme?

"So tell me, Neville. What happened to the ten lost tribes? You tell me you have a clue. You must! You have a sneaky grin on your face."

"David, I do. Although the nobility of the northern kingdom were mainly deported to Babylon, many were sent east to the Zagros Mountains to the lands of the Medes and the Persians. I believe they became a vital part of that culture. The Book of Esther serves as a clue. In that book, Vashti, the first queen of Xerxes I or Ahasuerus, as he is called in the book, refuses to disrobe herself during one of his long, drunken banquets. He removes Vashti as queen and invites maidens to become members of his harem. Ahasuerus falls in love with one of them, Esther, and marries her. He does not know that she is of Jewish descent. As we discussed earlier, Haman, an advisor to the king and spokesperson for the Persian nobles, plans to kill all the Jews. Esther comes to the king and tells him she is Jewish and will be one of those who are killed. He supports her when she tells him of Haman's plan. In the end, it is Haman and his family who are destroyed.

"But listen carefully what I want to share with you. It is what I found in the caves in the mountains east of Shushan. There was a partially demolished tablet that had a narrative on it that was never included in the Book of Esther or even in the Greek Apocryphal Book of Esther. Maybe the Jewish theologians did not want to add this to the history of that era. Maybe they did not want to admit that the Persian kings had Jewish blood. I do not know why. But listen to what I found after deciphering and memorizing the cuneiform message on the tablet. This is what it said:

"In the fifth year of our Great Lord and King, I approached him with great temerity for I knew that I was with child. And I fainted for fear of death from Haman's plan and from the heaviness of my condition. I told the Great King of my situation, and he was most happy to have another heir to the throne. It was then that I told him of Haman's plan to kill my people and me. He told me to plan a feast whereby Haman would fall into a trap and hang himself. I pray to Yahweh that I carry this child to fruition and that my people be saved."

M.S.PLATT   THE LAST SUPPER

"Well, David. I did more exploring. I proved by radioactive carbon dating that the tablet did come from the time of Esther, and I learned that Esther gave birth to several children. Among these were Prince Arsites of Persia, Amytis, Governor of Babylon, and Arsemes, Governor of Egypt. Artaxerxes I who reigned from 475 to 424 BCE was the first born of Ahasuerus/Xerxes I and Amestris. This was the Greek name given to Vashti.

"So, David. Where are the lost ten tribes of Israel? They are the breed of the Israelites, then and now, who assimilated with the Persians and the Medes. Who did not follow the code of Moses but the code of Hammurabi. They became the great Persian Empire that, in turn, was conquered by the Greeks, then by the Byzantine Roman Empire, and eventually by the Muslims. And these are the same people who are in this constant struggle between the Sunni and Shia. These control the commerce of the black gold of oil and threaten the world with sophisticated atomic weaponry and terror. These are the ten tribes of Israel! And somehow, by an ironic twist of history, they are now the adversaries of Israel. How will I get this message out to the world when I cannot even get a simple concrete tablet out of Iran? Maybe that is the reason the Iranians did not want the tablet to get into other hands."

Neville shrugged his shoulders and lamented. "You know, David, I had that tablet in my hands, but I can do nothing about it. How am I going to let the world know about these amazing historical events? How?"

I embraced Neville and comforted him. "Neville. Be patient. The truth will come out. Maybe Kristin, your wife, can help us disseminate the truth. Let's wait 'til next week when she comes, and we will discuss it with her.

"But it is getting late and we need to board our plane for Israel. I look forward to a happier time tomorrow when we can enjoy the visit with my family."

We ran to the boarding area and took our seats. The plane took off easily. The flight was quiet and peaceful as the humming jet engines sedated us, and I fell asleep immediately.

CHAPTER II

I was awakened by the announcement that we were approaching Ben-Gurion and looked out the cabin

M.S.PLATT   THE LAST SUPPER

window. The plane banked sharply exposing the afternoon sun adorning the landscape. And I saw a pleasant land, a fertile land, enriched by sparkling cities and busy highways, and polka-dotted brown hills crisscrossed by iridescent irrigation streams. I remembered that today was Palm Sunday, and I wondered what it was like to be in Israel two thousand years ago. I wondered what it was like on that Easter Sunday, and what it would be like even now. I felt a lump in my throat, and I asked myself how could this gentle land, this fertile land, this land of 'milk and honey', be so turbulent, so fraught with danger and mistrust, so hostile to its inhabitants these past three thousand years. And a tear dropped onto my quivering cheek.

Neville began to stir, and I gently nudged him. He also was viewing the land from the window but did not speak, for he was awed by the view. I assumed that he also knew that this was Palm Sunday. We both gained a glimpse of the Judean foothills approaching Jerusalem. Did not Jesus come on this very day to this city on a young donkey? Had not the people greeted Him, and laid clothing and palm leaves in His path? He came in peace, not on a horse or chariot, symbols of war. He came to preach, and the people viewed Him as Zechariah had promised: the Messianic King of Israel. He had come to preach His message to the multitudes in the Temple who had gathered to prepare for the Passover. But here, He did not find the Temple a place to worship God. Instead, He found chaos and disorder: animals for sale and moneychangers who bartered gold and silver so that these people could buy the animals. He upturned the tables of the merchants, the moneychangers, the dove-sellers, and He chastised them that they had turned this sacred Sanctuary into 'a den of thieves'.

"Hey, Neville. We are here. Ben-Gurion is just ahead." The plane made a gentle approach towards the runway and came to a stop. Then it restarted and moved to the terminal door. We heard the usual recitation by the steward advising us to stay in our seats until we were safely parked. Each passenger looked at his or her neighbor ready to enjoy a stay in the Holiest of Holy Lands.

"Hey, David, Passover doesn't start until Tuesday night. What do you suggest we do?"

M.S.PLATT   THE LAST SUPPER

"I think we should relax and enjoy ourselves tonight. First I need to call my family here in Tel Aviv when we get in the airport. I think that they must be preparing their house for Passover. That means cleaning the whole doggone place by removing any chametz or uncleanliness related to leavened bread products. They have separate dishware and pots and pans. Even the oven gets a cleaning. So I guess we ought to let them alone for today. We can stay at a hotel and meet them tomorrow. Besides, I am exhausted and need more sleep. There are several hotels in their neighborhood. They live in a quaint old part of Tel Aviv called Neve Tzedek. It is in the southwest part of town near the Mediterranean. Maybe we can even walk to the nearby beach. My family was lucky. They bought this dilapidated old house years ago when that part of town went downhill and property could be bought cheaply. Now, that part of Tel Aviv has been gentrified. There are plenty of restaurants and shops and expensive high-rise apartments. I am sure that we can find a place to stay tonight."

"Tell me about your family, David. How are you related?"

M.S.PLATT   THE LAST SUPPER

"These are my cousins from my father's side. His family stayed in Lithuania when my great-grandfather moved to the United States. My great-grandfather's sons stayed in Vilna, a part of Lithuania that contained many pious and Talmudic Jews. The Nazis utterly destroyed that area. A few of my family fled to Russia during the Polish invasion of 1939. These survived the holocaust. After the war, all the remaining Jews were invited to immigrate to the new state of Israel so they moved here in the late 1940's. Some even took part in the 1948 War of Liberation. By the way, Neville, I need to ask a favor of you. Some of my family from Vilna did not escape to Russia and were killed in Treblinka, one of the concentration camps that the Nazis used to gas the Jews. So please don't bring up World War II or anything about the war during our visit. It is still a sad part of our family history."

"I understand, David. I'll be careful. I still remember the stories my father told me about the Battle for Britain and the air raids when he was a kid. Well, we are now parked at the terminal gate. Let's get our luggage and make our calls."

M.S.PLATT   THE LAST SUPPER

The disembarkation from the plane was very measured. The Israeli airport agents made contact with every passenger. Each visitor was interrogated so as to make sure that no terrorists entered the country. My passport was examined, then my baggage. I was asked many questions, but since I was from the United States and a professor at a U.S. university and my papers were in order, I got through the lines without much difficulty. Neville had adequate papers and identification because of his work in archeology. The investigator seemed to know him so Neville got through the lines faster than I did. We met in the main hallway and gathered our bags.

Neville called his wife in London and told her that we had arrived safely. After some quiet romantic chatter, he turned to me and suggested that I call my family. In fact, I was already in that process.

"Hello, Abram. Hello. Shalom. This is David from America. Wanted to let you know that I have arrived safely and am at the airport. I brought a friend with me from Britain. ...No. Not a wife. It is a male friend that I knew in college. ... Well, we thought we would stay at a hotel tonight. You need to get your house in order for tomorrow. ... Now, now, you are very kind... I assumed that you have adequate room for us to stay with you tonight, but we don't want to impose on you. ... But we can stay in a hotel in Neve Tzedek and be no bother to you. ... Yes. Yes. I know you are insisting that we stay with you. I tell you what. I'll discuss it with my friend, and I will call you back. I have your address. Is it Derech Neve 9? Is that correct? We are going to get a cab and go down to Shabazi Street, have a bite to eat in a neighborhood café and then I'll call you back. Thanks for your offer."

"Well, Neville, he insists that we stay with his family tonight. What do you think?"

"I need food. I need a drink, David. I need to separate myself from moments of anger and frustration. Let's get a cab like you said and make a decision later."

We got a cab outside the airport grounds and told the driver to take us to Neve Tzedek. The cab turned into Route 1 toward Tel Aviv. Neve Tzedek is in the southwest part of Tel Aviv. It was the first Jewish neighborhood outside of the old port of Jaffa and had even preceded the founding of Tel Aviv by twenty-five years. At first it prospered with low-rise buildings and long narrow streets. Artists and writers made it their

M.S.PLATT   THE LAST SUPPER

home, but by the late 1940's and early 1950's it degenerated into disrepair and decay. It was to be demolished to make way for fancy apartments and modern highways but was saved by conservationists who resisted those plans. Renovation of the old buildings preserved its history. Restaurants, cafes, and coffee shops, theaters and schools, boutiques and elegant high-rise apartments gave a rebirth to the area.

 We traveled off the freeway into Neve Tzedek and passed Independence Hall on Rothschild Boulevard where David Ben-Gurion recited Israel's Declaration of Independence. We then proceeded onward to Shabazi Street that had many of the restaurants and cafes. We first spotted an ice cream shop and an Italian gelateria, but Neville wanted something more substantial so we requested the driver to drop us off at a cafe with sidewalk tables. At these, there were many customers, and the atmosphere was light and joyous. A waiter greeted us warmly and handed us a delicately flowered menu. I ordered a vegetarian meal of bell pepper salad followed by grilled eggplant and a glass of Golan Heights Chardonnay. David ordered a falafel appetizer and shrimp in a buttery citrus and garlic sauce with a glass of white Riesling.

Neville wondered how he was able to order a serving of authentic shrimp in an Israeli restaurant when this dish is clearly contrary to kosher or kashrut law. The answer was that Jewish restaurants in Israel adapt to a variety of international tastes. Some maintain kosher rules and are inspected by the rabbinate. These restaurants will usually serve only dairy and vegetable foods so as to avoid the conflict of mixing dairy with meat products, a dietary restriction, at the same table. Others, in order to address diverse international tastes, are not inspected by the rabbinical councils and are not advertised as being kosher. Neville did enjoy the shrimp!

Now our stomachs were full, and we decided to take a short walk down Shabazi Street to the Neve Tzedek beach and its promenade. The Mediterranean resembled a slowly moving cloud as a rainbow of afternoon colors danced on the shallow waves of the water. Not a ship or person could be seen, and we felt alone and isolated, yet safe from the troubles of the land. But it was time to move on, so I called my cousin and I advised him that we would soon be on our way.

The house was not far from the Shabazi Street restaurant and the beach. Using a local map, we traveled through some small alleys and pathways to find it, and as we walked, I could picture what Neve Tzedek was like in its earlier days. The house was on one of these pathways. It was a modest home with a waist-high, open metal fence surrounding a courtyard and a luxuriant garden. The entrance to the gateway revealed two, sideway, twelve-inch high, stone lions. The home was two stories high with a Mediterranean tile rooftop. Its outside was painted with yellow and white mosaic patterns where renovations had taken place. A small red brick path led from the gateway to a red front door. Irises, tulips, Madonna lilies, and hyacinth had grown during the wet November to February rainy season and abundantly populated the courtyard. Pink and white cyclamen and red, white, and purple anemones intermingled with the flowers. These all emitted a faint sweet fragrance as we walked along the path. A not- yet-blossoming honeysuckle vine clung upon a single tall palm tree that stood at the front and to the right of the house, and a few songbirds serenaded the day chirping away as they stood on the bushes of the various flora.

We approached the door. Midway, and about five feet from its bottom, was a doorknocker that embellished a massive lion's head. Its edges were fringed with verdant hues of oxidized copper, and above it was a small peephole that was used to observe any visitors--or worse, any hostile parties-- as they approached. Along the right of the doorpost hung a mezuzah, a metal framed, semi-oval receptacle that enclosed scrolled inscriptions from Deuteronomy 6 and 11. These reminded the faithful from Deuteronomy 6 that "The Lord, your God is one; Love the Lord your God with all your heart, with all your soul, and with all your strength." And from Deuteronomy 11: "Be careful or you will be enticed to turn away and worship other gods and bow down to them. Then the Lord's anger will burn against you, and He will shut up the heavens… and you will soon perish from the good land."

I knocked on the doorknocker and soon heard the firm footsteps of the owner. The doorknob turned and before me stood a middle-aged man with black, curly fringed hair along the sides of his face and fully displayed upon his head. He was straight statured, but his abdomen showed a faint bulge over a ballooning shirt and wrinkled trousers.

"Shalom! Shalom, he cried and welcomed us into the house. The main front living room was a step-down. It contained a green ottoman couch and soft red and tan chairs along its edge. Paintings from Israel and beyond were arrayed along its walls. The ceiling was of prickly cement covered by pink and yellow hues. The room's interior was quiet and inviting. Soon behind him came a young matron of his age and two children, a boy of about twelve and daughter of eight. They were dressed in clothes typical of western Europeans and Americans.

"Come in! Come in", my cousin exclaimed. "You must be exhausted. Are you hungry? Anna here can prepare something for you."

"No," I replied. We just got back from a restaurant, but we could use some more sleep. I had been up most of the previous night on the airplane and still have jet lag. Neville, my friend, was up all night as he waited for me at Heathrow. Are you sure you have room for us. You know, we could stay at a hotel."

"No. No." We have room, but it may be a little tight. Your friend can sleep on this couch in the living room, and I have a couch upstairs in the library that you can use. This is Anna, my wife, and my two children, Isaac and Rebecca. We have spent the whole day getting the house ready for Pesach. Tomorrow you can have a wonderful Israeli breakfast although there will be no bread. But enough to satisfy you."

Anna prepared the couch in the living room for Neville. I followed Abram upstairs to the library where a prepared couch was awaiting me.

Abram turned to me. "Get some rest. We can talk in the morning. We have a big day tomorrow ahead of us." He closed the door of the room and left. I threw my bags on the floor and jumped onto the couch, unkempt and fully clothed, and fell soundly asleep.

CHAPTER III

I awakened about 10 o'clock the next morning, still groggy, but ready to embark on the activities of the day. The sun beamed through a small window, and I was able to look about the room. On the previous evening, I had been too exhausted to do so, and the room was poorly lit. Now in the bright sunlight, I was amazed to see that the walls were stacked with books from floor to ceiling. Books lay haphazardly upright and on edge. Pieces of paper with multiple notes intervened between many of the books. As my eyes adjusted to the scene, I was able to discern the diversity of the reading matter. This was Abram's library, and I was immersed in the depth of this man's intellectual exploration--and it was diffuse and expansive. Not only were there worn copies of analytical studies of the Hebrew and Christian bibles, I was now able to discern books dealing with Arab thought and religion. There was a worn copy of the Qur'an and others dealing with Sunni and Shiite religious practices. There were even several historical documents that explored the Ottoman Empire's expansion into the Middle East and the Balkans, as far as Venice and Vienna. I now realized how well Abram was versed with the political, economic, and religious dynamics of this part of the world. I also knew that he appreciated the relationship of the Muslim world with Christian and Hebrew history and traditions. I found the Tanakh, a text that contained the entire volume of

Hebrew scripture, in addition to the Talmud in Hebrew and English editions. There were books dealing with the history of the Israelites before the Exodus to Babylonia as well as books on Jewish wisdom and the mysteries and evolution of the Kabbalah. It was now that I gained a deeper, healthier respect for this man. He was the Everyman of this household, and no less a man than any in my history department in Boston.

I rose to get washed up, for I wanted to meet him and explore his agile mind. I walked to the door but heard a knock.

"Who is it?" I asked.

"Anna… Are you awake, David? It is getting late. I bet you are quite hungry by now, and I have prepared a delightful Israeli breakfast which your friend Dr. Hudson is already enjoying."

I put on a light robe that was near me on a chair, ran to the door, and opened it ajar. I thanked Anna and promised to become presentable shortly. She was correct. I *was* quite hungry! After a quick shave and shower, I dressed and danced down the steps to the main floor where I spotted Neville assailing a plate of eggs, fruits, and vegetables. The food was on paper plates since I assumed that the Passover kitchenware had not yet been brought out. Passover would begin on tomorrow evening. I did not find Abram in the room so I asked Anna if he had gone to work.

"No," she replied. "Tomorrow is Passover Eve and all the men of the family have gone to the Synagogue to prepare. In ancient times, at the time of the deliverance from Egypt and slavery, the Hebrews sacrificed an unblemished lamb and placed its blood on their lintels and doorposts. God promised to destroy the firstborn of all the Egyptians and their animals, but would "Passover" the homes of the Hebrews. Thus, originated the Hebrew term "Pesach" or in English, "Passover." Since the time of the destruction of the Second Temple in 70 CE, the Jews don't sacrifice a paschal lamb. Instead, we have fasted on the morning of Passover Eve in commemoration of the Lord's salvation of the Hebrew firstborns on the night of Passover. But now the men just go to a ceremony at the Synagogue, pray, read some passages from the Torah and have a celebratory breakfast. They are preparing for tomorrow's breakfast and should be back soon. They can join you and Neville, but I am sure their appetites are satiated. Eat your fill gentlemen, for this morning we are going to put you to work for we need to burn all the remaining chametz that we find in the house. I will get you a flashlight and a feather duster so that you can check the storeroom and closet shelves. By the way, if you find a locked closet, do not be confused. We lock up some chametz items like our liquor in these closets and sell them to the Synagogue, who in turn, sells them to some of our Arab and Christian friends for the week of Passover. Then we buy them back and reuse them after the festival. Sounds like fantasy, but we do all of this so that the house is considered chametz- free."

Anna pointed to the table. "So David, what would you like for breakfast? I have some hard-boiled eggs, orange juice, tomatoes, cucumbers, and green peppers for a salad. Or if you like, there is a dish of olives, another of salmon, and one of sardines. I have strong coffee or tea, but there will no bread or pastries because of the chametz issue."

I poked Neville on his arm. "Good morning, Neville. Hope you slept well."

"Quite well, David. Join me in some breakfast. This food is fabulous."

M.S.PLATT   THE LAST SUPPER

We ate a bountiful meal and took a short walk in the courtyard garden. Traffic on the narrow street in front of the house was sparse. Apparently, other Israelis were preparing for the holiday season.

Neville and I were still exhausted from our plane trip and the jet lag so we spent most of this day sleeping and eating lightly. We awoke the following morning, Tuesday, more refreshed and eager for the Passover festivities. Abram and his son Isaac had just returned from the Synagogue, and Anna handed each of us a flashlight and feather duster to complete the final search for the chametz throughout the house. Later in the morning, the kitchen stove was to be heated up to "maximum" so as to remove or burn off any remaining chametz in its interior.

This interlude gave me an opportunity to inquire about the massive library that Abram had collected. "Abram, that is an impressive library that you have upstairs. I took Neville upstairs to see it, and we were extremely impressed with your scholarship."

"David, Israel has been in the bosom of world history for over four thousand years. It has been geographically situated in the right place or wrong place, or, as some may view it, at the right time or wrong time of history. But Israel has shared its tragedies throughout history. This history has challenged us all to learn how we, as a nation, have succeeded or failed. We need to appreciate the conflicts and tragedies that have occurred here and to try to avoid them. To do that, one must learn our own and our neighbor's cultures, for only then can we gain insight into their lives, their motives, and differences. Only then can we learn to seek accommodation with them, if that is ever possible. If not, the wars and atrocities will continue. That is not what I want for my children."

"I agree." Neville added. "I wish all the peoples in this world had that attitude. The world would be a safer place. But for today, what can David and I do to help you this morning?"

"Well." Anna interrupted authoritatively. "You and David can repeat getting rid of all the remaining chametz. You need to do a better job." And she shoved the flashlights and dusters into our hands again and pushed us into one of the closets. When we had finished with that chore, she was waiting for us and pointed toward a large dining room table that had been set up in the center of the room.

" That is much better. Now, you can help me and Abram set up for tonight's Seder. Bring in some chairs from the other rooms for all the guests. See these boxes on the floor. They have the Passover utensils and dinnerware. We need to wash them and set up the individual places. I will show you how.

"Abram, do you have the napkins and glasses ready?"

After everything was washed and dried, Anna instructed us to set the table. In its center was a large dish. The dish contained a shankbone; some parsley leaflets; a small dish of horseradish; a second small dish of charoset made up of chopped apples, nuts, and honey, mixed with red wine and a roasted egg. The plate represented the symbols of the festival. The plate was then covered with a moist linen cloth so as to keep the items fresh.

Another plate was placed on the table. It contained three matzos, an unleavened flatbread. These were covered with a dry linen cloth to keep them fresh. Matzo is one of the main symbols of this festival. The Torah commanded that it must be eaten during the entire week of the festival. It symbolized the fact that the Hebrews left Egypt in great haste such that there was no time to allow any of the bread to rise. The matzos preserved well in the long journey in the desert. Matzo is made under strict religious rules and guidance. It is guarded against any fermentation and does not contain any leavening. It is made solely from flour and water. The dough can be rolled continuously by hand or machine but for only a short time, usually 5 minutes, when the flour and water are mixed so as to prevent fermentation or rising. A cutting instrument is run over the dough just before baking to prick any bubbles so that the finished product will not puff up.

  A third dish was then placed on the table. It contained salt water for the dipping of some vegetables during the proceedings of the evening. A fourth plate contained multiple sheets of matzo that would be consumed during the meal.

  In addition, each place setting had a wine cup, a pillow on each seat for reclining when eating, and a booklet called a The Haggadah. This booklet described the proceedings that would take place. A cup of wine to honor the Prophet Elijah was placed at the end of the table. On an adjoining table, a fresh bottle of sweet Jewish wine was placed. Portions of this would be consumed during the meal. On another adjoining table, Anna placed two candleholders with unlit candles.

    Abram advised Neville and me that the patriarch of the family, Grandfather Ari, would explain the meaning of all these items during the course of the evening. Now everything was all set, and Abram needed to pick up Grandfather Ari from the neighborhood home for the elderly. Grandfather was in advanced years and needed special supportive care, so he no longer lived with Abram and Anna. However, his old room on the main floor always awaited him. The main floor also had rooms for Isaac and Rebecca, the children. Abram also needed to pick up four more guests--Shlomo Leibowitz, his wife Leah, and their two sons, Aaron and Dov.

    Within an hour, Abram had returned with Grandfather Ari and the Leibowitz family. Grandfather was in his early nineties and walked with a slightly bent position. He had a short, well- manicured, gray-white beard and some balding at the top of his head upon which he wore a white skullcap. His face was adorned with many fine wrinkles about his forehead and chin, yet his arms were full and solid, and his trunk was enveloped in a black suit jacket and brown sweater. His blue eyes were still alert, and, as he entered the main room from the outer courtyard, one could see that he eagerly wished to meet the new guests from America and England. Abram brought him forward to greet us.

"Zedah. This is our long, lost cousin from America, David." David, meet Zedah Ari who is related to the grandfather of your father who immigrated to the States." One could see a wisp of a smile upon the lips of the patriarch of the family as he inched towards me. I could see him examine my face searching for any resemblance of the family line in my features, and I lunged towards him and gave him a warm hug, almost lifting him up in the process. I turned to Neville and introduced him to the patriarch. They shook hands politely. At this time, Grandfather seemed tired and sat quickly and firmly on an adjacent chair. The other guests were now entering the room so Neville and I turned to greet them.

Shlomo Leibowitz entered first. He was a middle aged modern Israeli with cleanly shaven face, medium height, and dressed in a relaxing tan sport coat and white shirt that was open at the neck. His hands were delicate as if he did not do manual labor, but instead, could have been actively engaged in the banking or software/electronics industries that were now bourgeoning in this land. Leah, his wife, was about his same age, neatly dressed in a flowered dress—appropriate for the spring-like atmosphere of this day. There were two boys, aged eight and six. Aaron, the elder, was tall and thin, with blond, short-cropped hair and brown, intense eyes and eyebrows. Aaron was the ideal candidate to ask the four questions that are historically framed to the patriarch on this night. His brother, younger and more docile appearing, was short and slightly obese. He walked with a slow, purposeful gait and appeared less interested in the people in the room. He seemed to touch various fixtures as he moved about, and he did not communicate with anyone.

It was now approaching dusk and since the Israelites have always considered the new day to start by the presence of the first stars in the heavens, Passover was soon to begin. Each person was assigned a seat about the elegantly laid Passover table. Grandfather was assigned the head position, Abram sat at the opposite end. Anna approached the two unlighted candles on the adjacent table, and chanted a prayer as she lit them and placed them in the candleholders.

"Baruch, Attah, Adenoi…Praise you, O' Lord, Ruler of the Universe, who makes us Holy by your Mitzvot and commands us to light the festival lights."

A second prayer followed.

"Bless you O' Lord, our God, Ruler of the Universe, who has kept us alive and well so that we can celebrate this special time."

Thus, the Seder, which means the order of the proceedings for the evening, could begin.

Grandfather poured some sweet wine into his cup and the others followed. He then chanted a prayer.

"Bless you O' Lord, our God, Ruler of the Universe, who creates the fruit of the vine." This was the first order of the evening—the Kiddish. There would be four cups of wine to drink this evening. Each would invoke the promises that God had made to the Hebrews when they left Egypt as recorded in Exodus 6:6-7. Each promise symbolized that:

1. I shall take you out from under the burdens of Egypt.

2. I shall deliver you from slavery to them.
3. I shall redeem you with an outstretched arm and with mighty acts of judgment.
4. I shall take you to Me for a people, and I shall be a God to you.

Grandfather then took a cup of water that stood by his chair and poured it over his hands, allowing the water to fall into an adjacent basin. Everyone was then given a leaf of a bitter vegetable, and they dipped it into a dish of salt water that was on the table and recited a prayer. This act reminded the participants of the harshness of slavery during the 400 years that the Israelites were in Egypt. The salt water reminded them of the tears of their labors and distress. Then each took a bite of the bitter herb.

Grandfather then took the middle matzo that was on the plate of three and broke it in half. He put the larger portion in a white cloth and would use it later in the service. The smaller portion was returned to the original plate. He reminded everyone that matzo was the bread of poverty that the ancestors ate in Egypt.

This was to be followed by the reading of the "Maggid," the retelling of the Passover story. But before doing so, he invited Aaron, the elder son of Shlomo to ask him the classical four questions that are framed at each annual Passover Seder.

Aaron approached Grandfather's side and smiled for he knew what the questions were and had practiced them prior to coming to the service. Historically, one of the questions referred to the offering of the sacrifice of the paschal lamb, but as noted earlier, that was not done since the destruction of the Second Temple. The question would be replaced with another so he began with the now traditional recital:

"Why is this night different from all other nights?"
("Ma nishtana ha lala hazeh?")

1. On all other nights we eat bread or matzo; on this night we eat only matzo?
2. On all other nights we eat all kinds of vegetables; on this night we eat only maror/bitter herbs?
3. On all other nights we do not dip our vegetables at all; on this night we dip them twice?
4. On all other nights we eat our meals in any position; on this night we eat leaning on pillows?

M.S.PLATT THE LAST SUPPER

The answers to these questions are addressed in the Haggadah, the text that grandfather shared with each of the participants. The answers were as follows:
1. Matzo is eaten for the seven-day festival in order to remember the Exodus from Egypt 3000 years ago.
2. Bitter vegetables are eaten to remember that slavery was hard.
3. The vegetables are dipped in salt water to acknowledge the tears and hard work of slavery.
4. The diners recline on pillows because the people were now free from slavery and could eat in comfortable positions as a free society.

The Haggadah also expounded on the ten plagues that are described in Exodus, the travels and the challenges of the Hebrews in the desert, their moments of resistance to the Commandments of God, and how the Jews had became a chosen people. The Torah was to be the pathway. It was given to the twelve tribes at Mount Sinai on the Pentecost, the fiftieth day after leaving Egypt. The Torah provided the standards that God had set for this chosen people. These standards, especially the Ten Commandments, were not only for them but would influence many generations of other societies and cultures from that era until the present day.

In some households, other children would also ask the four questions. They ranged from a wise child, a wicked child, to one who is simple and one who is unknowing. However, this concept was not egalitarian in the home of Abram and Anna and was not adopted.

Following the retelling of the Passover story, a second cup of wine was drunk to recount the Exodus. Then there was a second washing of hands and a blessing prior to eating any other food. Before eating the Passover meal, horseradish and the charoset were then placed on two pieces of matzo to make a sandwich. These were then eaten to remind the participants that the mortar that was used during the hard slavery was composed of straw.

Only then could the Passover meal begin. It consisted of an:
1. Initial helping of gefilte fish accompanied by a small helping of horseradish,
2. A cup of matzo ball soup,
3. Cooked or roasted chicken with potatoes and vegetables.

4. And followed by a dish of prunes and raisins.

Notwithstanding all this food and the length of the evening, the children remained alert for only then could the surprise following the meal take place. The "surprise" was the search for the second piece of matzo that was hidden from them. This piece was called the afikomen and was considered the dessert for the evening. In older times, some considered it the Paschal Lamb. Only if this piece were found would the children be treated with candies, nuts and other rewards. Aaron found it under one of the living room couches and returned it to Grandfather. Since Grandfather was an egalitarian fellow, all the children shared in the rewards.

Following this festivity, Grandfather chanted a blessing after the meal. Then he poured a third cup of wine and Hymns were recited.

Following the Hymns, Grandfather drank a fourth cup of wine, and opened the door to allow the Prophet Elijah to enter, for Elijah is the messenger of the coming of the Messiah.

But to Neville the notion of a Messiah meant another thing:

M.S.PLATT   THE LAST SUPPER

For memories are the mosaics of our yesterdays. As Neville watched the family partaking in the latter portions of the Seder, he remembered his own family partaking in the meanings of the Advent Season, Palm Sunday, and the Holy Week. He thought of the breaking of the matzo and the taking of the Afikomen, and he thought of an earlier Passover Seder, the LAST SUPPER. And he remembered that Jesus took the Afikomen, broke it, blessed it, and gave some to His disciples, and said, "This is my body given for you; do this in remembrance of Me." Then he remembered the third cup of wine, the cup of redemption. Jesus took the cup, blessed it, and said, "This is the new covenant in my blood, which is poured out for you." And he knew that in the minds of Christians everywhere that Jesus, the Messiah, had already come and now the door was opened for His second coming.

CHAPTER IV

So the Passover Seder had concluded, but the evening had not. The tables and chairs were quickly cleansed and items put away. The young people went to their bedrooms on the first floor to enjoy the sweets and well-earned rewards, but the adults, including Grandfather, relocated to the living room. Although, in previous times, families would discuss the Torah or the Mishnah Tractate Pesachim, in this household they planned to discuss Israel and its relationship to the modern world. Each of us slipped into the comfort of the soft cushions of the couch and chairs, the better to digest the heavy meal.

I spoke first. "Abram and Anna, Neville and I want to thank you for your hospitality and wonderful meal tonight. I am so glad that I flew to Israel to visit with you. I have so many questions. Abram, I am not always sure of what I read in American newspapers. So tell me. How goes it in Israel?"

Abram shook his head as if undecided how to answer. Slowly he began. " After over eighty years of statehood it goes." Then silence.

Leah interrupted. "After almost eighty years it goes with difficulty. Here we find a Jewish state, a place of haven for all the Jews of the Diaspora, even the holocaust. And what have we? It has been said that the Second Temple was destroyed because the Jews could not live peacefully with each other. They did not unify the country in order to deal with the Romans, and the Jews of that era had hate in their hearts, not love. What do we have today? Ultra-orthodox Jews, the Haredim, impose their laws on the rest of us. Shlomo and I go to a Reformed Jewish Synagogue. We were originally married in France by a Reformed rabbi. Does the Israeli Rabbinate recognize our marriage? Does the Rabbinate recognize any of our converts in our synagogue? I do not know. I do not know."

Then Shlomo chimed in. Our French culture had a large element of Sephardic Jews from North Africa. These Jews were, at one time, the most intellectual of the Jewish world. When these were attacked in their native homelands after the Arab uprisings, Israel welcomed them, and they came in droves. But now we have clashes between Ashkenazi Jews from Eastern Europe and the Sephardic and Mizrahi Jews from North Africa, Alexandria and Algiers. I am a banker and I find myself in a major argument whether Israeli currency should have a photo of an Ashkenazi Jew or a Mizrahi Jew on its face. People forget that Mizrahi Jews have Turkish and French cultures and many come from the metropolitan areas of Istanbul, Alexandria and Algiers.

M.S. PLATT   THE LAST SUPPER

We can be as sophisticated as any of the Eastern European Jews."

Leah then added. "There is even tension between the orthodox and conservative and reform movements in Israel. Only Orthodox Judaism is officially recognized in Israel for the purposes of performing religious marriages, divorces, and conversions. Even burials. Our synagogue receives minimal government funding, and we cannot hold services at the Western Wall of the Second Temple. The Kotel. We are ostracized because women participate in our services. We believe in an egalitarian congregation where women and men are treated equally, but at the Kotel, we are not equal partners."

Shlomo added. "And the Haredim, the ultra-Orthodox, are even exempt from military service in the Israel Defense Forces. Only recently did the Knesset pass legislation that enforced drafting these young people, but it was watered down, and all the criminal sanctions were lifted. Only five percent of Israel's Jewish population above the age of 20 is ultra-Orthodox, yet they dictate what commerce may take place on the Sabbath, what stores may stay open."

"Yes." Leah joined in. "And they marry young, have multiple children, sometimes six or seven. That causes severe stress on the national economy because they get financial support so that they can stay at home. And their men never work. They study Torah at their nearby Yeshivas."

I turned to Anna. "Anna, what do you think?'

"Well, David. It is true that some of the Haredi Jews reject Zionism. They believe that national political independence can only be achieved through the intercession of God and the Messiah. And they wait for that day. Look up one of their positions papers. I believe you can find it on the Internet under the term "Neturei Karta." You will find that they believe that Zionism is influenced by socialism, and that socialism looks upon religion as an outdated relic. They believe that the true essential nature of the People of Israel is found in the Torah. Without Torah, there is no People of Israel. The purpose of the People of Israel is Divine Service. This is the only salvation for the Jewish people. Zionism is materialistic and contrary to the notion of divine service. Zionism represents the State and Army of this nation, but service to the Creator should be the function of the whole world. In fact, David, they believe that the Torah forbids the end of the exile of the Jews. Only the Holy One can redeem the people. They believe that most of world Jewry should live in the security of the foreign nations wherein they live presently, and Jews should have no desire to live in a Zionist state."

So I turned to Leah. "Well, Leah. Do you think this will ever change? Can the political climate of Israel change these circumstances?"

She laughed out loud. "I doubt it. Look, David. We are a nation that has over ten political parties. Recently the law was changed such that any political party was required to represent at least 3.25 % of the population before it could submit candidates for election to our legislature, the Knesset. Did that reduce the number of parties? No! And the Knesset has 120 seats so any political party needs a majority of 61 seats in order to form a working government. In years past there were two major parties—Labor and Likud. Now these have been diluted because politicians gain popularity and split from their parties and organize even more splinter parties. No party gets a clear majority so it needs to bargain with other parties in order to gain a balance of power and form a government. Now come the religious parties. Many of them are not run by a central committee, but are controlled by prominent rabbis. Any party that seeks to form a government must court these religious groups so, in the end, the religious groups have held significant sway over the politics of the nation. This has been true since 1948 when the nation first declared independence. Religious authority was granted to the orthodox elements, while public institutions such as the army were granted to the Zionists. This has always been referred to as "the status quo." The religious are, at times, even at odds with the Supreme Court of Israel. This court does not base its rulings on religious policy. Several years ago a pro-religious Minister of the Interior was advised by the Court that he must recognize reformed and conservative converts to Judaism."

  Shlomo pursued the issue. "David, did you know that more than 50 % of the ultra-Orthodox live below the poverty line compared to 15% of the rest of the population? Did you know that there is no public transportation on the Jewish Sabbath? The Chief Rabbinate must certify any restaurant that advertises as kosher. Importation of non-kosher foods is prohibited. No civil marriages are allowed in Israel in spite of freedom of religion."

Here Grandfather Ari joined in. " Now. Now. Shlomo. You must admit that the ultra-Orthodox do provide emergency medical attention at suicide bombing scenes and grant free loans of medical and rehabilitative home-care equipment to members of all faiths. And it does so without any government funding. And don't forget that 80% of European Haredim perished in the Holocaust. And yet, Judaism does not condone violence. It demands that Jews be good citizens of the country in which they reside. The Talmud tells us that God obligates us not to rebel against ruling bodies; therefore, not to take the land of Israel by force. Zionism presents as an aggressor that takes this land from its indigenous inhabitants. Remember—the State of Israel under its Zionist government tramples on the religious rights of its inhabitants when it performs autopsies on its people, when it rips open sacred burial grounds in order to build commercial malls. Zionism and its adherents claim to be a replacement for Judaism. Is that true?"

M.S.PLATT   THE LAST SUPPER

Abram realized that Grandfather Ari had forgotten that he was a remnant of East European Jewry that was saved by these same Zionists. He forgot that these Zionists had fought for the establishment of this state so that Ari could move here in peace. So in deference to Ari's age and patriarchal status, Abram decided not to pursue these discussions and change to another topic.

"So tell me. Should we be concerned by the high unemployment in our country? Does it not threaten our economic future? Look at the national statistics. The Jewish population is now approaching 7 million people. That is 75 % of the Israeli population and 43 % of the Jews in the entire world. The 2 million Arabs in Israel account for 21% of the Israeli population. By 2025, the population of Israel will be almost 10 million and it will have a growth rate of 2%. But the Jewish growth rate will be 1.7% while the Arab rate will be 2.2 %. Will the Arabs overtake us or will the high reproductive rate of the ultra-religious prevent that? They have 3 to 6 children per family. The Jewish and Arab populations are composed of young people, but our older people are growing in number. How will we cope with that especially when our economy is slowing down? Our economic growth rate is only 2.3% and I am not sure where it will go if there is a worldwide recession.

"Even now it is reported that 1 % of our 30 to 54 year old Israelis is not even looking for work! Our young people are having difficulty finding stable employment and job security. Prices continue to rise especially in the housing market. Many cannot find affordable housing. Thank God we bought this house many years ago when prices were lower. I have heard that some young people are returning to the United States and Canada because they cannot raise a family easily in Israel."

Shlomo interjected. "As a banker, I can tell you. The government is not spending enough money on infrastructure. There is excess capacity and less demand in the market. That is what happened in the depression of the 1930's. And government inaction is making things worse. The economic growth of the country is not equitably distributed. I have seen money channeled to politicians, rich people and their families. So the young people become more right wing leaning, and the peace process becomes even harder. The slowing of the economy filters down to the Arab population. They do not work or make a decent living, and they are becoming more hostile and aggressive. I worry that they will join Hamas. I fear that they will support Iran in a missile crisis, even atomic war."

"Shlomo. Don't be so pessimistic," Leah exclaimed. "God forbid that should happen!"

"I don't think it will come to that." I suggested. "The United States has been a valuable ally to Israel. The U.S. has offered financial, military, and political help to Israel for over 50 years. It provides over $ 4 billion a year in military aid and up to $ 9 billion in loan guarantees. It considers Israel a strategic ally in the Middle East."

"But it stopped giving us economic aid in 2007," Shlomo complained. "Claimed that we had a robust economy and did not need that aid."

I volunteered, "But the U.S. does offer military financing as long as Israel spends 75 % of the aid on U.S. defense equipment. Don't forget that American taxpayers pay for that aid as well as for the loan guarantees."

"But, David." Abram interjected, "the U.S. can take away that military aid as it did in 2009 when it imposed a virtual arms embargo on Israel and turned around and gave the Arab states $ 10 billion in arms."

M.S.PLATT   THE LAST SUPPER

"Do you think the fact that Israel continues to push for settlements in East Jerusalem and the West Bank might be a factor?" Neville asked. "These settlements anger the Arabs and adds to mistrust of the motives of the Israeli government. There are over 320,000 Israeli settlers in the West Bank and East Jerusalem now. Will that ever end?"

"Maybe these are in response to the U.S. government statements that Israel should return to the pre-1967 borders." Abram rebutted. "Maybe these are a response to the influence of the ultra-religious politicians who placate their constituents who want Israel to occupy the entire Palestine. I do not know, but these issues could be resolved if the Arabs would accept the notion that a Jewish state in Palestine is a finality. What do you expect Israelis to hope for when Hamas and Iran take the position that Israel must be wiped from the surface of the earth? The issues of settlement, borders, return of displaced Arabs during the 1948 and 1967 wars are negotiable, but they are not negotiable if the Arabs want to destroy us."

"Abram," Neville responded, "I heard when I was in Iran doing some archeological studies that the Arabs are not too happy that Israel has high density nuclear bombs at the Dimona nuclear facility and won't admit it or allow the installation to be inspected. And they are not happy that the United States supports Israel with numerous vetoes in the United Nations debates. They argue that the U.S. cannot be an unbiased partner in peace treaty negotiations when it uses these vetoes in defense of Israel. I was told that they believe that the occupation of the West Bank and East Jerusalem is an invasion of Arab lands and a violation of international humanitarian law. It seems to breed more anti-Semitism and terrorism. I am also aware that a conservative group in the United States called 'J Street' supports the notion of an end of the Arab-Israeli conflict through dialogue."

"Well, Neville." Abram retorted somewhat angrily. " If the Arabs who you are talking about would just accept Israel as an equal nation in the Middle East, I am sure some dialogue could begin and the frictions of the parties in this cauldron of bitter hostility can move forward to a peaceful resolution.

"The partition of Palestine is not a recent issue." Abram continued. "It has festered for over one thousand

M.S.PLATT THE LAST SUPPER

years. When the Muslims conquered the Holy Land in the 7th Century, they did not plan to give it up so easily. They European Crusaders first came to retrieve the land but were expelled by the 13th Century. The Jews began to buy land in the 1850's and lived at peace with their Arab neighbors for about 50 years. Then the Western powers expelled the Ottoman Empire in World War I. The Balfour Declaration of 1917 supported the establishment of a Jewish Home for the Jewish people, and the Mandate of the League of Nations in 1922 ratified that notion. But the lure of oil in the region and greed of the Western nations put an end to that. The Arab riots of 1920, 1929, and 1936-1939 sealed the doom of a Jewish state in Palestine. The Peel Commission of 1937 tried to negotiate a partition, but that approach did not gain agreement by any of the parties. The British White Paper of 1939 limited Jewish migration and land purchase in Palestine, and that mollified the Arabs. When the horrors of the holocaust in Europe became evident, the hope for a homeland for the Jews was renewed, but the British were unable to deal with the migration of the homeless Jews of Europe. The United Nations passed a partition plan in 1947, but the Arabs rejected it. They claimed that the Jews received too much land in relation to the Arab population. A war ensued and the Jews were able to keep much of the land attributed to them by the United Nations. The war left ugly scars. Casualties occurred in both ranks of the combatants. Palestinian villages were destroyed. Many of the Palestinians fled the area and remained in refugee camps for many years, and this fostered hostility. Of course, it was the Arabs who attacked the Jewish settlements in the Jewish allotted lands, but the Jews succeeded in driving them off. A truce was reached in 1948 and Israel declared its independence. No agreement has resolved the refugee situation or the ownership of land evacuated by the Arabs. The Arabs attacked again in 1967 and lost more land. The Arab position has been that Israel has no right to exist. Only Egypt and Jordan have accepted the nation's existence. My friends, that was and is the situation, and I do not see any evidence of a change of heart by any of the parties. Is there any hope?"

"Well, Abram," Neville responded. "I can see why you have some anger, but how about looking at the Arab point of view? Where is justice for the Arab people? Did not the prophet Micah tell the Jews in Micah 6:8: 'He has told you, O mortal, what is good; And what does the LORD require of you but to do justice and to love kindness, and to walk humbly with your God?' ".

Neville's face looked strained, and he continued. "The reason I say this to you all tonight is that I am an archeologist and I have traveled in Arab lands, and I have heard things that have disturbed me. I need to share these things with you. Lets look at some of the Arab frustrations.

"First, there has been discrimination against the Arabs, and this takes place in Israeli controlled areas. Arab housing has been demolished. Only a limited number of building permits have been issued, so Arabs can't rebuild their homes. Arab towns in the Galilee have been isolated so that social and economic continuity is compromised. Look at the justice system. Arab defendants are denied bail and, when adjudicated, obtain longer sentences and prison terms. This is just not what I have been told. Look at the U.S. State Department Country Reports.

"And look at education. Israeli schools get three to ten times the amount for education. Arab school classrooms are overcrowded, and the dropout rates are higher. Arab students have lower college admissions, in part, because they do not easily pass the Psychometric Entrance Exams. As a result, only 5% of civil servants are of Arab origin when 20% of the population is Arab.

"Look at the distribution of land. The Jewish National Fund or JNF has taken over "absentee land", that is, land that Arabs escaped in the 1948 and 1967 wars. And the JNF does not lease other lands equitably to Arabs. If an Arab leaves his home in East Jerusalem or the West bank, he may lose the right to return. In fact, the issue of the right of return of Arab refugees after the 1948 war has never been resolved.

"Look at the economic dilemma. If the economy of Israel decreases, it affects the Arab economy even worse. Public funding erodes, and tax benefits to stimulate business disappear. Arab men and women don't gain any employment.

"Water rights for the Arabs have not been discussed. These conflicts only cause more mutual distrust and increase the level of violence between the parties. There is a need to agree on fixed borders for the two independent states. Arabs are concerned that some

M.S.PLATT   THE LAST SUPPER

Israelis still dream of a greater Israel as described in the Torah. The Torah described Israel as a land extending from the river of Egypt to the Euphrates. If so, then the West Bank and Jordan would be included. This notion needs to be repudiated by Israel and the Zionist organizations. Well, have I made my point?"

    Abram realized that the evening would continue for an inordinate period of time, and he noted that Anna and Leah were beginning to dose off. He also noted that Grandfather Ari was now sound asleep on the Ottoman couch. He turned to Anna and suggested, "Anna, it is getting late and you and Leah have had a long day. Why don't you cover Grandfather with a light blanket so that he can sleep on the couch and you and Leah go to sleep in one of the bedrooms?"

  "Abram, you are right. We are not going to resolve these problems tonight. Leah and I are going to sleep in Rebecca's room, and we will see you all in the morning. Goodnight!" Anna covered Grandfather with a light sheet and the two women exited the room.

  Abram now turned to Neville. "Neville, some of the points that you have made are well taken, but the problems you discern are deeper. Let us look at the notion of partition. This problem has been smoldering even before 1948. Start with the Muslim invasion of this land in the 7th Century. It remained Muslim territory until 1918 and World War I. Yes, the Crusaders recovered some of the land and Jerusalem, but they were expelled by the 13th Century. From the 15th Century on, the Ottoman Empire controlled this land. Yes, some wealthy European Jews contributed funds so that agricultural and urban projects were negotiated with Arabs starting in the 1850's, but the Jews were a minority and conflict was minimal. The Zionist movement in Europe in the late 19th Century opened a new door. When the Ottoman army retreated from Palestine, the British issued the Balfour Declaration in 1917. That document established a National Homeland for the Jews in Palestine. The League of Nations restated this concept when the Palestine Mandate was created in 1922. The British and French divided up Mesopotamia, Iran and Palestine when the Ottomans, represented by Turkey, signed peace treaties after the war. Alas, the indigenous Arabs were not about to give up the Muslim dominion of these lands. The Arabs instigated riots against the British and Jews in Palestine

M.S.PLATT   THE LAST SUPPER

in 1920. These were repeated in 1929 and became unmanageable when more Jews came to Palestine after the Nazi Germany attacks on Jews after 1933. The Royal 'Peel Commission' offered a plan for Palestine partition in 1937, but the Zionists and Arabs could not agree on its terms. An Arab revolt ensued from 1936 to 1939, and the British issued a White Paper in 1939. This document restricted Jewish immigration and land purchases. The Middle East remained somewhat quiet during World War II although the Arabs did cooperate with Germany and Italy. However, the British army took complete control of the Middle East during the war. The Jewish holocaust during World War II by the Nazis sounded a new call for a Jewish homeland, and Jewish immigration to Palestine increased. The British could not control the adversities that ensued, so the United Nations suggested a partition of Palestine in 1947. A war ensued. The Arabs invaded Jewish areas, but the Arabs could not reclaim all the land. The Arabs invaded again in 1967, but lost the West Bank and East Jerusalem. The Arabs complained that the 1947 partition gave the Jews 56 % of the land when the Jews were only 1/3 of the population and owned only 8 % of the land. They complained that the 1948 war resulted in the destruction of many Palestinian villages and that 70 % of the Palestinians became refugees in other lands. They demanded 'a right of return' to Palestine. These confrontations as well as the occupation of the West Bank and East Palestine caused greater hostility. UN resolutions for peace and return of the refugees went unheeded. Arab terrorism during the Intifadas of 1987 and 2000 only made matters worse. But, Neville, the problem is even vastly deeper.

"Perhaps a review of the history of the Middle East might give some clarity of why the Arabs do not ever care to give up the control of these lands. The Middle East, the 'fertile crescent of civilization' has never been the cradle of peace and civilization that it claims to be. If one examines the history of this area, it has been the route of marauding bands of peoples from the deepest of Africa and the steppes of Asia for as long as humankind has walked on this earth. Written history can begin with the Persian Empire that existed until 323 BCE. This empire extended from India to Greece, but Alexander the Great and his Greek armies conquered it in 323 BCE. Alexander died in the Indus River area while pursuing his conquests so his generals divided up the spoils. One general took the western lands extending from North Africa to Syria, and the other took the eastern lands. The eastern Seleucia Empire continued until about 64 BCE when nomadic tribes from Asia minor overtook the Greek dynasties and formed the Parthian Empire that lasted for 400 hundred years until 224 CE. The Parthians adopted many Greek cultural elements and peoples, but civil war ended their control. Turkish nomads formed a Sassanian Empire and conquered them about 224 CE. This civilization extended from Pakistan to Arabia and served as a vital link in the trade routes from Asia to Europe. It even defeated some Roman advances. It was originally tolerant when it favored Manichaeism religious practices, but became intolerant when it adopted the Zoroastrian religion. Alas, wars between the Sassanid Empire and the Roman Empire, called Byzantine by that time, had eroded the strength of both. The Bubonic plague that also developed at this time did not help either.

'"In the 7th Century, Muhammad, the Prophet, nurtured the Islamic religion. Within one hundred years, Islam extended from Spain to India and China. How were the Muslims able to do this in so short a time? It is assumed that the Sassanid and Byzantine wars and internal strife weakened these empires. In addition, Jews and western Christians unhappy with Sassanid and Byzantine governance and religious practices welcomed the Muslims. The Bubonic plague took its toll. And, clearly, the religious zeal, cohesion, and mobilization of the Muslims acted in concert to achieve these victories. But the Muslims did one other thing that cemented their acceptance by the conquered peoples. The Muslims were unmerciful with any communities that resisted them, but they were gracious with any that surrendered without a battle. The Muslims even agreed to allow the enemies to practice their religions as long as these peoples paid a tax."

  Then Shlomo joined in the discussion, "The conquered lands were also aided by social and economic contributions by the Muslims. The Muslims were bold. Many Arabs from the Arabian Peninsula migrated to the conquered lands. Their leaders were of the merchant classes, and they cooperated with the local elites, formed cities and retained the agriculture that was in place. Truly, they were open to other religions and social orders. They assimilated with the people, but problems arose. The conquered people learned that if they accepted Islam, they would not have to pay heavy taxes, so they assimilated with the Arabs. Taxes became unbearable so the Arabs required that no one could convert unless they studied the Qur'an and was circumcised. Higher taxes and suppression were then applied on the Jews and Christians in their communities. Class stratification by wealth and power ensued. Friction within the cultures took place."

"And the emergence of two wings within the Islamic faith added more friction," Abram added. "When Mohammad died in 632 CE, he left no male heirs. A dispute arose over the question of succession. One group believed that leadership should fall to 'a person who is deemed by the elite of the community best able to lead the community.' The majority of the Muslims took this position and prevailed. They were called the Sunni and chose the first Caliph. A smaller group—the Shi'ites or Shia-- claimed that someone from the Prophet's family should succeed. They favored Ali who was married to Mohammad's daughter Fatima. Ali was chosen as the fourth Caliph, but war erupted in 661 CE. The violence and the wars caused a split in the Arab Muslim faith into two entities that would never reunite. The Sunni now make up 85 % of the 1.5 billion Muslims; the Shi'ites make up about 15 %. Most of the Muslims that live in Turkey, Egypt, Jordan, Syria, northern Iraq, and Saudi Arabia are Sunni. Most of the Muslims that live in Iran and southern Iraq are Shi'ites. Mixed populations of Sunni and Shi'ite live in Yemen, Oman, UAE, Qatar Kuwait, Pakistan, Afghanistan, and the West Bank. The problem was heightened by the fact that Ali's son, Hussein, rejected the Sunni Caliph. The Shi'ites called their leader Imam, and Hussein was the third Imam. Hussein was killed, and the Shi'ites commemorate his death every year. The Imams have taken on a spiritual significance that no Sunni cleric enjoys. In fact, the Sunni believe that the Shia attribute divine qualities to the Imams, and that is a great sin. To Sunnis, only Allah is God. In the 10th Century, the 12th Shi'ite Imam went into occultation. The Shi'ites believe that God took the 12th Imam into hiding, and he will come back as a Messiah or Mahdi. Those who believe in the Hidden Imam are known as Twelver Shi'ites; and they are the majority of the Shi'ites in the world. They believe that the full word of the Qur'an and the Prophet will become manifest upon the return of the Mahdi. Unfortunately, there have been periods of conflict between the Sunni and Shi'ites, and the split remains. Muslim theology rules that Muslims not fight with each other unless one threatens the other or is a heretic faith. That is exactly what happened in 1507 CE when Selim I of the Ottoman Empire accused Shah Ismail I of the Safavid Empire in Iran. Intermittent wars ensued for almost three hundred years until 1847 CE."

Shlomo interrupted. "Gentlemen, I am getting quite sleepy, but before I go to bed, would you tell me why there has been continued disagreement and tension between these two sects?"

I responded. "Maybe it has to do not only with faith but to other things. Think of political power and control of the world market on oil. Most of the oil is in Shi'ite territory in central Iraq, Iran and Kurdish lands even though the Saudis have massive oil reserves. In addition, the Sunnis and Shi'ites differ in doctrine, ritual, law, theology and religious organization. The Sunni extremists and jihadists as well as the Islamic

State of Iraq and Syria (ISIS) consider the Shia as heretics who should be killed. And consider, when the Iranian revolution was launched in 1979. The Shia agenda supported use of Shia militia and sectarian conflicts. Perhaps the execution by Saudi Arabia in 2016 of a Shia cleric was considered an example of this conflict. Before you go to bed Shlomo, let me remind you that Iran was Sunni at first, but in about 1500 CE, the Safavid Dynasty took over Iran and changed its religion to the Twelver school of Shi'ite Islam. So, Shlomo, let me ask, what is a Shi'ite Arab? Different authorities define an Arab by language, geography, culture, and religion. Iranians speak Arabic, but their religion and geography are clearly not Arab. Contrast this with the Ottoman Empire that derived from Turkish tribes in Anatolia/Asia Minor from about 1350 to 1450 CE. The Ottomans are Sunni, and they had been in conflict with Shia Safavids for two hundred years. They interfered with the trade routes of the Safavids, conquered all the lands in the Middle East except that of Iran, and controlled the Holy Land until World War I."

 "Thank you, David. Thank you all," Shlomo exclaimed. Although this has been a most enlightening evening, I need to go to bed. I think I will join the boys in their room. Wake me early in the morning please."

Abram picked up the conversation. "David, that is not all. I need to share with you and Neville what I think goes on in an Arab mind, what goes on in a Jewish mind.

"Since I am Jewish, I think that I should start with what I think constitutes a Jewish mind. First, the Jews are the People of the Book—the Torah, God's Law, the roadmap of God's relation to humanity. It is the pathway to God given to Moses by God. Secondly, the Jews are the People of the Land. It is the Land granted by God to the children of Israel --a promise by God -- a place of inheritance. And when expelled from the Land, it became a place of yearning, a place needed, a place of return. The essence of Judaism is the Torah. This document signifies man's duty to God and to his fellow man. It specifies that the Jews were the chosen people-- to love God, to recognize Him as a single deity and to serve Him. The Jew is committed to study the Torah, to learn from it, and to seek one's relationship to God. Thus, the Jew learns to read early in life, to study early in life and to probe his relationship to God. This endeavor promoted the development of a judicial mind, but, at the same time, it put the Jew in conflict with others, with himself, with his neighbors. When the Jews were expelled from their Land, they had to undergo the rigors of an alien in alien lands. This was their Diaspora, and they had to acclimatize to their conflicts as outsiders, learn the ways of others, but were restricted by the tenets of the Torah. From the Greeks, the Jews learned about the discipline of philosophy; from the Arabs, the mastery of mathematics, language and science; from the Italian Renaissance, the beauty of secular reality; and from the Enlightenment, the expansion beyond social and cultural barriers. Yet the Jews of the world were diversified by their geography, and one Jew could be vastly different from another, save for the teachings of the Torah and the Talmud that was added to the Torah during the Diaspora. The Jew could be described as cunning, sly, or crafty, but he was none of these. Instead, he was studious, intellectual, cerebral, and rational. He was a reflection of his travels in the Diaspora, but, at the same time, anchored to his Torah, the teachings of his forefathers, and his duty to his God. The Jew of the Land of Israel is grateful that he has returned to his Land but fears that he will be confined to a ghetto in his Promised Land, or worse, be threated by extermination in this Land. The Jew of the Diaspora still deals with the conflicts and challenges that affect his growth in an alien Land, but hopes for survival and salvation in order to carry on the Jewish faith.

"So how do I feel about the Arab mind?" Abram now hesitated. "Let me think for a moment.... Yes. The Arab is also a People of the Book, a Book granted to him by the Prophet Mohammad, a book that tells him of his relationship to God and humankind. He is also a People of the Land, a land acquired by conquest. Yet it is his second home, for Mecca and Medina are his first home. Jerusalem is his second home, for Mohammad visited here. Palestine is the land of Muslim power and glory in history. It is a land of interaction with the Jews for 1400 years. It is a place where they adopted notions of one God, elements of the Jewish bible, and a similar restrictive diet. Know this, my friends--the Arabs are a tribal, kinship people who are generous and hospitable, and they show courage and power of a true warrior whenever necessary. Yet they show the character of patience, hard work, and grief in times of adversity. But they have a deep self-pride in themselves and do not easily admit to error or failure. Thus, the Arabs view the loss of Mesopotamia and Palestine after World War I to the British and French and the division of these valuable lands and the oil riches that lay beneath them as a catastrophe. In the Arab mind, the British and French are guilty of colonizing the Arabs, and this is an oppressive idea to Arab culture. Similarly, the loss of Arab lands in the 1948 and 1967 wars is a matter of loss of face, of shame, to them. Thus, they will wait patiently until they gain in strength and will return to reclaim their lands.

"But their culture suffers, for they have difficulty in dealing with modern science, freethinking, and access to knowledge. Their women are oppressed and at times treated as second-class citizens.

"I feared when the Arab nations explored Pan-Arabism in the 1960's and 1970's and courted relations with the USSR; but, fortunately, those experiments failed. I do worry now about recent relations with Iran and Russia."

Abram continued, "The Arabs and the Jews both want and need this land. Can this land satisfy the needs of one state with one mind or as two states with separate minds? In my heart, I believe that the Jew of the Decalogue, the Jew of the Ten Great Commandments, can live in peace with his fellow Jew and with his neighbors in his Land. And I believe that the compassionate Arab, the Arab who tolerated the religious practices and mores of those lands that were conquered ages ago can live in peace with his fellow Arab and with 'the stranger in his Land'. Only then will the 'lion live in harmony with the lamb and live in harmony with God's one eternal plan'."

David interrupted. "I could not have put it better, Abram, but if you two can excuse me, I also need to go to bed. I will be in your library on the second floor if you need me. Plcase call me early in the morning as you do with Shlomo." I quickly disappeared upstairs.

Neville turned haltingly to Abram. "Well, Abram. I guess that leaves only you and me here tonight. It is getting quite late, but I need to share some more thoughts with you before we go to bed. And that is the indefensible positions that the United States and the Western powers have maintained in recent conflicts in the Middle East. Let me start with some pro-Western writers. They were enamored by Kemal Ataturk's conversion of Ottoman Turkey to a modern secular state in 1922. And they argued that all the Arab lands should become democratized. Unfortunately, the need for continuous sources for oil and the greed of the Western powers caused resentment in the Arab world. Pan-Arabism was the response to Western intrusions. Think of the seizure of the Suez Canal by England and France in 1956 and the interference of Iran's oil interests by the United States in 1953. Some political advisors in the United States promoted the 'balance of power' concept whereby the U.S. would prevent the emergence of any regional single power that could monopolize the flow of oil. Pan-Arabian nationalism was a response to that notion, but it was replaced by the tyrannies of dictators in Syria, Iraq, and Lebanon. Fundamentalist terrorism followed as dictators tried to maintain their hold in power. In time, the oil cartel was a response to U.S. positions."

Abram countered. "But Neville, didn't the Iranian revolution of 1979 appear to leftist college professors and their captivated students that there would be the formation of a new democracy in the Middle East? It is unfortunate that the leftists were proven wrong when the Iranian State became an oppressive theocracy. After that blunder, the U.S. embarked on shaky, ambivalent relationships with Pakistan and Saudi Arabia, but none of these states embraced laissez-faire economics, cultural pluralism or political democracies. Perhaps Muslim countries cannot contemplate the separation of religion and state."

"Perhaps," Neville responded, "but it is time that the Western countries begin to consider suggestions made by pro-Arab analysts. According to them, the U.S. missed the mark. These analysts maintain that after the Ottoman Empire was split up in 1918, a link with the Arab world was severed. The West went one way, the Arabs another. Yet I believe that there may not really be a 'clash of civilizations' between the Arabs and the West. There may *really* be a place for both—for Islamic *and* Christian cultures. The Arabs look to Islam to constrain the corrupt tyrannies that presently exist in their countries and hope to return to the center of public life in a solid base of Islamic values. They assert that the West should refrain from devaluating Islamic education and Islamic law, or marginalizing Islamic scholars. The Arabs need their religious parties to hold bona fide parliamentary elections. The West needs to respect the Arab clerics. Give Arab clerics in Iraq a chance to champion the Iraqi underclasses. Give the moderate clergy in Iran a chance to promote verbal discourse. It may take a generation or two. After all, Europe and Christianity struggled for years to resolve the role of religion in civil society. Even in the United States today fundamentalist religion and government are at odds. The United States Supreme Court is called on constantly to pick up the pieces of that controversy. So I think that "Arab Exceptionalism" is a good idea. Give it a chance. Islam is not anti-modern."

"But, Neville," Abram asked, "I am still concerned. Will the competing ideologies of the Sunnis and the Shi'ites permit this to happen? Will these two offshoots of the Prophet Mohammad flood the oil markets? Try to overwhelm each other? Try to gain knowledge and expertise in atomic weaponry? Will they attack each other or the Western nations first? Or, God forbid, even Israel?"

"I doubt it, Abram. Give the Arabs…"   "What was that?" Neville felt a rumble. "Do you have earthquakes in Tel Aviv? What is that noise?"

M.S.PLATT   THE LAST SUPPER

"Neville. It sounds like a fleet of airplanes or, worse, bombers coming in. Listen."

But it wasn't bombers. The noise became increasingly louder and closer as they listened. Soon it was joined by sounds of crashing debris and rushing waves of water. The earth continued to shake, and the foundations of Abram's house lost it's mooring as the waves of water crashed into it and demolished its walls. The water reached as high as six feet and engulfed Neville and Abram and swept them away. Both men were driven against the disrupted walls of the room and into the outer courtyard and streets, each one trying to swim and fight to stay alive.

CHAPTER V

It appeared that the whole western edge of Tel Aviv was engulfed by the Mediterranean Sea. Abram's house and its foundation could not be found. The destruction extended for about two miles inland. Was this an earthquake? A tsunami?

The emergency services of Israel were quickly alerted to the catastrophe. Searches were extended inland and about the sea and its shores. Interestingly,

M.S.PLATT   THE LAST SUPPER

the land south of Tel Aviv, in Gaza, was less affected, but Jaffa and its port were demolished. There was much loss of lives and property, and many lives were not only drowned by the onrushing waters but also pulled out into the sea as the waters and debris receded towards the Mediterranean.

   I was apparently the fortunate one, for I was soundly asleep on the second floor couch, innocently oblivious to the ongoing cacophony. The crashing of the walls of my room startled me and brought me to my senses. Although I was confused by the noise and darkness, I soon recognized that my couch was water-borne, carried away out through a breach in the wall of the second floor and onto a rushing river of water. The couch seemed to act as a small boat that was buoyed on the surface of this river and carried me inland with the waves. My body hurt as the walls crushed my arms and legs while traversing the breach. Blood began to run down the side of my face, and I noticed a deep tear of my flesh on my scalp and sideburns. I began to feel numbed and in shock, but remained alert enough to realize that I was being propelled inland. Then there was a sharp lurch and the couch—my boat—came to an

M.S.PLATT   THE LAST SUPPER

abrupt stop in a ditch of mud and slime. The acceleration of the couch caused me to fall forward into the deeper aspects of the ditch, and I lay there motionless, not knowing if I was alive or if I could recapture what had happened to me in this brief moment of terror. Where was I? I was too disoriented and in shock to fathom the circumstances. I tried to explore my body and noticed that there was a cake of mud and debris from my head to my ankles. I tried to brush aside some of the larger portions of the debris and mud and crawled forward onto some adjacent, firmer, safer terrain. And I lay there motionless, almost breathless, and in awe of what had happened in so brief a span of time. I could not easily talk for mud was plastered in parts of my mouth and began to cough and spit out the material. If I had swallowed any of it, I shuttered to think of the biological repercussions of the ingestion of any human waste. I just lay there for an indeterminable period of time in the dark, in this wasteland, hoping that someone would rescue me.

Soon I heard some distant voices, and tried to call out, but it was difficult for me to do so. In time the voices came closer, so I grasped a piece of debris and threw it in the direction of the voices. They heard the thud of the dropping debris and turned toward me.

"Anybody there?" they called out, so I threw another object at them. They turned toward me and recognized that I was a limp body needing help. One of the emergency persons came to me and began to pull me to safety onto a medical stretcher. Another worker began to cleanse my face and mouth of mud. A third person brought some water and removed some of the mud from my torso.

"Who are you?" one of them asked. "Where are you from?"

"Thank God you found me. I am David Adams from the United States. What happened? Where am I? I was visiting with friends in Neve Tzedek for the Passover Seder and went to bed. Next thing I know, I'm here in this damn ditch. What the hell has happened?"

" Just relax, my friend. We'll get you to a hospital and get you some medical care. Thank God you are alive. You are on Ben-Gurion Street in Tel Aviv, a good two miles from Neve Tzedek. It appears that there was a tsunami that engulfed the beach and inland parts of Tel Aviv, and you were dragged here by the water."

M.S.PLATT   THE LAST SUPPER

"Where are my friends? Are there any survivors?"

"Can't tell you. We are searching for survivors. Most of the area of Neve Tzedek and the beach has been lost. I don't know if there are any survivors, but we are looking for them. We need to get you to a hospital to see if you have any broken bones or serious injuries. We'd better get some dressings on that cut on your scalp and face before it gets infected. Are you allergic to any medications? Here, let us help you into an ambulance."

I was transported without delay to Rabin Medical Center, farther inland, where I was re-evaluated again. Fortunately, I did not have any broken bones, just the lacerations on my face and scalp. These were cleansed with antiseptic solutions and redressed. Then I was put to bed where I rested for several hours. A nurse approached me later that afternoon. "You have an important phone call from London, England. Will you take it here?"

"Yes, of course. Who is it from?"

" A doctor. Kristin Hudson. Will you take the call?"

"Good, God. Neville's wife." And grabbed the phone.

"Kristin. Have you heard... have you heard about the tsunami here in Tel Aviv?"

M.S.PLATT   THE LAST SUPPER

"Yes, David. The British Tele stations are now reporting it. That's why I am calling. Where is Neville? I have tried to reach him by cell phone, but I am not getting any responses. I'm worried. Is he with you?"

"No. I lost contact with him last night. We were visitors at my cousin's house in Neve Tzedek. It is near the beach in Tel Aviv. Good God. I was found two miles away and brought to a hospital. How did you find me?"

"The Magen David Adom, the Jewish Red Cross, has been searching for family members. I told them that I was looking for Neville Hudson and that he was with you. It was then that I was advised that you were in a hospital, and they would connect me to you. Oh, David. They don't have any record of Neville. I hope they find him well. I don't know what to do..." Kristin paused. "David.... in fact, I do know what to do.... I am going to cancel the rest of my lectures at the University and fly to Ben-Gurion in the morning. I will get a cab from the airport and meet you in the hospital. How are you doing? I hope that you do not have any serious injuries."

"Kristin, believe it or not, I only have a laceration of my scalp and face. And several bruises on my legs and arms. No broken bones. No water immersion injuries.

M.S.PLATT   THE LAST SUPPER

Would you believe that the paramedics found me two miles from the beach? I am lucky to be alive! Look, come as soon as you can. The authorities are searching for survivors. I will check with them as best I can and keep you posted by cell phone. I pray that they find Neville alive and well."

"Oh, David. So do I. I will see you in the late morning or early afternoon. I have an early morning flight out."

I lay back onto the bed. The bruises and the laceration were now beginning to hurt. I was given clear liquids to drink and a soft diet and slept for most of the rest of the evening. When I woke up, it was dark. I turned to a nurse and asked her to connect me to the Magen David Services. They advised me that Neville had not been found yet, but that they would still be looking for survivors in the waters off the beach and inland. Bodies were now being washed up onto the shore. I began to weep for Neville and fell asleep.

My bed faced the east so the morning sun easily breached the shades of my window. I awoke with a startle and with the hope that Neville would be by my bed; but, unfortunately, he was not. My hopes sank rapidly, and I waited for the arrival of Kristin later in the day. I still ached, but I was grateful that I was alive.

The nursing staff began to ambulate me, to force me to walk around the bed and room. With mixed emotions, I looked at the entrance of the ward, for Kristin would be coming, and I had no news.

At mid-afternoon I saw the motion of a woman approaching me. She was about 15 years junior to Neville's age, as tall as he was, and spotlessly dressed in a brown woolen jacket and skirt, mid-calf boots, and a head of brilliant red, kinky hair. Beneath her jacket she wore a diaphanous yellow blouse that showed a prominent protuberance of her abdomen. A thin silver necklace and bejeweled crucifix hung from her neck, the crucifix lying neatly tucked within the cleavage of her abundant, well formed breasts. She was astonishingly beautiful, and I could see why Neville had spent considerable time in romantic conversations with her on Abram's home phone and his cell phone. She was directed to my bed, and I sat up to greet her. Her mouth was pursed as if she wanted to ask me where Neville was, but she hesitated when she saw me alone. I arose from the bed and embraced her tenderly.

M.S.PLATT   THE LAST SUPPER

Kristin gave a gentle whimper, and whispered, "David, have you heard anything?"

"Kristin. Kristin. I am so happy you came. No. I've waited and waited. Not a thing. But I still have high hopes." We slipped onto adjacent chairs both resigned for any news, good or bad.

"Kristin. I heard that my cousin's house is missing. There is no house, only a washed out foundation. No one from my cousin's family has been found. None of the hospitals have any record of their admissions. They are presumed to be lost in the tsunami, but the searches continue. Bodies are being taken to mortuaries, where finger print and DNA studies are being conducted to identify any remains. I am sorry to be the bearer of this bad news, but that is the status of this catastrophe. I need to get you into a hotel and get you some rest. You must have been up all night."

"I have, David. But I don't want to get any rest. I need to carry on until we find Neville. I miss him so. Why did this happen? Why, to my beloved Neville?"

"I don't know either, Kristin. Look at the evening newspaper."

M.S. PLATT   THE LAST SUPPER

The newspaper reported that tsunamis actually strike the Israeli coast every fifteen years, but they are minor ones, with little damage. They are called Blue Tidal Waves. In fact, the Israeli Defense Department conducts emergency drills for them. The Department has a 30-minute warning system. The last major tsunami struck Acre in the 19th Century. Other tsunamis have struck Caesarea with gaps of 200 to 2000 years. They do occur in the Mediterranean Sea but usually are associated with earthquakes, volcanic eruptions, and landslides. In other parts of the world they may be caused by tropical cyclones. Some of the harshest tsunamis have occurred recently in Indonesia and Japan but have been associated with massive earthquakes, usually magnitude-9.0. The main tsunamis that threaten Israel come from earthquakes from the Crete-Greek Arc, southeast of Crete, and the Cypriot Arc southeast of Cyprus. Eight thousand years ago a volcanic eruption on Mt. Etna in Sicily led to a massive avalanche sending six cubic miles of rock and sediment into the Mediterranean Sea and triggering mudslides that flowed throughout the eastern Mediterranean. If that happened now, it would have traveled 450 miles an hour and caused waves 130 feet high. Israel would have been struck in 3½ hours. Nothing like that happened in this tsunami. In fact, the authorities were searching for an earthquake that could account for the present tsunami.

Kristin threw the newspaper to the floor in despair.

"David. You are right. We better settle down for a long wait. The answers will take some time. Do you know where some decent hotels are in this city?"

"No. I don't, but the nursing staff will help us out."

The nursing staff allowed me to check out as an outpatient. Kristin and I rented an auto and drove to a nice hotel in Petah Tikva, a community near the hospital, and we obtained separate rooms.

The news concerning the tsunami was disheartening. There was no gigantic earthquake in the Crete-Grecian Arc, or in the Cypriot Arc for that matter. Nor was there a massive volcanic eruption to account for this tsunami. If anything, it seemed to begin, disturbingly, a mere 90 miles north- northwest of Tel Aviv in the Levantine Basin, just in the heart of the Leviathan gas works of Israel. And its magnitude was a mere 7.0, quite insufficient, at the most. And more—there were few, if any, aftershocks that accompany earthquakes. So the evidence was meager to support the dynamics of this great catastrophe against the coast of Israel.

To be sure, the results were egregious. The number of deaths or missing rose to more than 80,000 and the property damage exceeded $180 billion, in part, because the property in the area consisted of prime expensive high-rises, hotels and new development. And the area was in the western coast of Israel, a land but 120 miles long and about 50 miles wide, a land that held a population of over four million people, 95 % of which were Jews.

Thus, the explanation of this catastrophe required more exploration and better explanation. The nation became dissatisfied with any banal excuses or hypotheses, and the investigations intensified. The Prime Minister was at a loss of words and the Departments of Defense and Interior were now taxed to the maximum. Israel looked to its neighbors for explanations, but there was nary a word from them. Not only a word, but a lack of concern, of caring, of support so as to deal with this holocaust.

M.S.PLATT   THE LAST SUPPER

Israel turned to the United States, its valuable ally in the West, and to Europe. From these, it received aid in the form of medical crews and materials. From the United States came expertise for the analysis of the phenomena of tsunamis and earthquakes and various dilemmas of this nature. But the true explanation of the event remained unresolved.

Then there was the issue of an earthquake. Was the initiating event an earthquake? Earthquakes arise because landmasses collide with each other, a phenomenon called tectonic plate theory. In these circumstances, a subducting plate of land pushes beneath and downward under an overriding plate that pushes above and in an opposite direction. These interacting plates are noteworthy along the Pacific Ocean rim and the North and South American and Asiatic continents. They also occur in the Mediterranean Sea and Middle East due to the collision of the African Plate drifting northward under the Eurasian Plate.

One of the most recent and significant earthquake-induced tsunami occurred in Japan in 2011. This magnitude-9.0 earthquake took place off the northwest coast of Honshu, the Japanese main island. It occurred

M.S.PLATT   THE LAST SUPPER

18.6 miles below the floor of the Pacific when the Pacific Plate subducted below the Eurasian Plate along the southeast coast. The epicenter of the quake was 80 miles east of Sendei, a community on the east coast of the nation. When the plates collided they formed a subduction zone 190 miles long and 95 miles wide. The zone lurched 164 feet toward the east and southeast, rose 33 feet and caused a horizontal and vertical thrust of the Eurasian plate. The plates compressed each other and became stuck for a variable distance at their intersection. The subduction zone became a region of immense potential energy, and the lower plate became exceedingly hot. In time, the two plates slipped apart in a violent fashion, and this massive energy became dissipated to the surrounding environment. The tremendous energy was transferred to the adjacent water so as to cause tsunami waves as high as 33 feet in height. One wave was known to have traveled 6 miles inland carrying debris, property and human lives. The waters then raced back to the sea. Other waves raced outward from the epicenter in opposite directions forming 12 feet waves and traveled to Hawaii, Alaska, and the west coast of the United States.

M.S.PLATT   THE LAST SUPPER

Earthquakes are measured by a variety of indices. One measure is the Richter scale. This scale does not measure quake damage but measures the amplitude or height of the largest seismic wave at a specific distance from the epicenter of the quake using various seismographs. A distance of 62 miles is usually chosen. The Richter scale is a base-10 logarithmic scale. That means that each order of magnitude is ten times more intense than the previous one. The amplitude increases 100 times between each level, and the amount of energy that is released is 31.7 times between the whole values of the scale. A magnitude-9.0 Richter is equivalent to a 20 trillion kilogram explosion of TNT. A magnitude-6.0 is equivalent to a 60 million kilogram explosion.

A more recent index of measurement of earthquakes is the moment magnitude scale (Mw). This is a measure of the size of an earthquake in terms of the energy that is released. It is valuable for large earthquakes but not for those that are magnitude-3.5 or less. This measurement was developed in the 1970's and has become popular since 2002. It is used for the larger quakes. It is based on the "seismic moment of the earthquake" and measured by the amount of slippage at a land fault and the size of the area that slips.

Obviously, nothing of this magnitude occurred in the Mediterranean Sea just north and northwest of Tel Aviv. The maximum Richter scale was only 7.0. So a quandary still existed. What caused the tsunami to inundate the west coast of Tel Aviv?

Time has a habit of moving rapidly when one wishes to savor the richness of life, but slowly when pain tears at the heart of the human soul. And so it was. There was no information or any identification of Neville; but there was an abundance of time to deal with the consequences of this trauma to Kristin, --to the nation of Israel, --and to me.

It was now Thursday. Kristin and I awoke early, eager to continue our search for more news. We had a light breakfast, and then contacted the Magen David authorities—but there was no word of Neville or my family. We were not allowed to travel to Neve Tzedek since rescue and search missions were still operating in the area. We were resigned to continue our search using our cell phones and the Internet. Fortunately, these services were still operative.

M.S.PLATT   THE LAST SUPPER

I began to feel more fatigued and my muscles ached. My bruises and the cut on my face did not help. A redness of my skin appeared on my arms and chest so I decided to return to the Medical Center for my daily checkup.

"Hello, Mr. Adams," the nurse greeted me. "Did you get a good night's sleep?"

"Somewhat," I replied somberly. "I'm still sore all over, but I now have a rash on my body. It sure itches. Do you think I was allergic to something in the mud that encased me?"

"Let me take a look." She examined my arms, then my face.

"The rash seems to be growing in intensity," I added.

"Hmm. Have you been in the sun at all?" she inquired.

"No. Not at all. What do you think?"

" Not sure. Maybe we should take your temperature. Have any fever?"

" Not that I know of. I don't have a thermometer."

She pulled out an automated thermometer from a near-by cabinet and inserted it into my mouth. We waited until it registered. Then she retrieved it and looked at the reading and advised me. "You don't have a fever. I will have a technician draw some blood and get a blood count. Any other symptoms?"

"Well, I did not feel like eating breakfast this morning. Maybe I'm a little nauseated. I feel like I want to vomit, but can't."

The tech drew my blood, and I lay down on the outpatient bed. I was really feeling more fatigued and nauseated. I spit up some vomitus.

The tech returned with the nurse. Both appeared somber and anxious. "Mr. Adams, may we call you David? You are a member of our family now."

"That is OK with me. What did you find?'

"It seems that the blood count needs to be redone. I am calling Dr. Bar Ilan to see you and explain."

After a short fifteen-minute delay, a short, stocky elderly chap approached me. I was beginning to feel more anxious, and what he told me did not allay my anxiety one bit.

"David, I am Doctor Bar Ilan. I feel badly that you are having these difficulties. Sometimes the automated blood cell counter makes an error. It is best that we redraw your blood and check your blood count."

"Well, doctor. Can you explain what my difficulty is now?"

"Well, David. Let's not jump at conclusions. I have the technician with me. He will draw another sample. Let me see your rash. Itching, you say?"

"Yes. And it is getting worse."

"Hmm. I see."

The blood sample was drawn again, and I settled back on the bed as the doctor examined my skin, throat, eyes, and everywhere that was externally visible. I waited with awe, but there was nothing I could do. I thought of Neville. Where would he be? Would Kristin and I find him? What was the rash all about? Why was I nauseated?

Dr. Bar Ilan returned quickly. "David, the tests were correct. Somehow you blood count is not normal. You have a low white blood cell count, and I need to check some more things." He retrieved a small box from his pocket and put it on my skin and next to the shirt that I was wearing. It made a few ticks at regular intervals, and I could see the register on a dial moving erratically. His eyes opened widely, and his face appeared concerned.

M.S.PLATT   THE LAST SUPPER

"David, Have you been near any nuclear facilities recently?"

"No, doctor. I just got here from the States a few days ago. What is going on?"

"Well, I will get some consultation. This apparatus is a dosimeter called a Geiger counter, and we are picking up some radioactive signals from your skin and your clothes. Apparently, you have had contact with some radioactive materials. Tell me where you've been and what you've done these past several days."

I re-iterated to him all that had transpired since I left Boston. He rechecked the signals from the counter and hurriedly exited from the room. On the way out, he turned towards me and exclaimed, "I am getting another colleague. Be back in a minute." He returned in ten minutes with another person.

"David, this Doctor Rosin from our Radiology Department. He wants to examine you. We need to get more information."

Kristin came to visit me, but when she began to enter the room, the nursing staff held her back. Then they checked her with the Geiger counter and found no signals. She was not allowed into my room. The staff conveyed messages from me to her and back again.

Somehow I had been in contact with radioactive materials since I had come to Israel. The authorities were sure of that fact. They needed to find out where. A company of nuclear medicine specialists soon surrounded me. I was stripped of my clothing, and these were put into special orange colored bags. My skin was washed with detergent solutions, and I was now isolated to my room. The specialists muttered to themselves and nodded frequently as they examined me. They began to look more anxious and disturbed as they communicated with each other. One of them pulled out a cell phone.

"Moshe. This is Eliezer at Rabin Medical Center. I have some disturbing news. We have a visitor from the United States. He allegedly claims to have had no contact with radioactive materials that he knows of. Please send some personnel to the Neve Tzedek area where the tsunami took place and check for any activity." The doctor then slowly closed his cell phone, looked to the ceiling, seemed to pray for a moment, and quickly exited the room.

M.S.PLATT   THE LAST SUPPER

"What is going on?" I anxiously asked. My nurse assured me that everything was under control. "Not to worry," she insisted. I could see Kristin in an adjoining room. She was nervously pacing around the room, and I became more concerned because of my personal status and because I wanted to know if there was any more news about Neville.

During the next three days I learned more valuable information. Apparently I was not the only one who had been in contact with nuclear emissions. The entire inundated coast of Israel had shown this same evidence. This information leaked out to the media, and the citizenry in Israel became hostile to the government because of what had happened. The source of the emissions was not clear, and that was the question at hand. The Department of Defense soon sent teams out to the coast and Mediterranean Sea to take emission measurements.

After I had been cleansed of any radioactivity of my skin, Kristin was allowed to enter my room, but she was required to use reverse isolation and to wear protective gear. One could hardly see her fine features. She wore a full fitting surgical gown, paper over-shoes, a facemask, rubber gloves, and a surgical cap to cover her hair. She looked forlornly at me. I was not sure if she was concerned about my circumstances or hers. There still was no word about Neville. I began to give up any hope of hearing from Abram and his family. Somehow they were lost as the waters receded back into the Mediterranean. However, search teams continued to ply the waters since bodies kept washing up on the coast daily. These would be moved to the local mortuary, examined, identified by fingerprint or DNA, and families advised of the retrieval of their loved ones.

On Easter Sunday, Kristin came to me in tears. She had wished that Neville would be identified. She shared a thought with me.

"David, when Jesus died and was buried, He returned on this very day, Easter Day, and was later seen by Mary and His disciples. I so wish that Neville would return to me. It would be another miracle." She put her face on my shoulder and repeated her prayer to me in sobbing whispers.

The days continued to pass. Ten days after Neville's disappearance, a person meeting his features was found on the shoreline, but after a complete analysis of the remains, it turned out not to be Neville at all. He remained missing and unaccounted for.

I myself was having my own dilemma. My white blood count continued to decrease, and I was in danger of obtaining an infection because my neutrophils, those cells that combat infection, were getting to a desperately low level. In addition, my other white cells, called lymphocytes, were dropping. One type of these cells, the T cell helper cells, was decreasing. It was like I had AIDS in which these cells decrease, but I did not have AIDS. I had acute radiation sickness! My skin condition was a lesser issue. It was my bone marrow. Bone marrow is that net-like structure within the core of my bones. It is the source of most of my blood cells and cell progenitors. And it was failing. The doctor advised me that I had indeed ingested some of the radioactive material as it was carried in the mud and water of the incoming sea. After I ingested these toxic products, they were absorbed by my intestinal tract and transferred to my bone marrow. The radioisotopes were now destroying the DNA of my marrow cells and killing those very cells that form my blood components. My white blood cells were attacked first. Then my red cells would decrease, and there was the danger of becoming anemic. Similarly, the cells that would form my platelets were affected, and when that happened, I was at risk of bleeding to death. What a terrible situation I was facing! These medical issues were addressed by transfusions to prevent anemia and medications to increase my white blood cells. However, since the stem cells, the progenitors of my white and red cells were being destroyed, these did not respond to the medications, and I found myself relying on frequent transfusions of blood and of white cells and platelets to keep me alive. I required antibiotics to ward off infections, but using these, as a pre-emptive approach was meaningless, perhaps misleading, because the bacteria in my body would become resistant to the various antibiotics that I was given. Now I was at risk of attaining blood stream infections or pneumonia from these antibiotic resistant bacteria. And then, no antibiotic would save me.

   The investigative authorities from the Defense, Interior, and Health Departments eventually ascertained that the tsunami originated in the region of the Levantine Basin north-northwest of Tel Aviv and directly west of Haifa. An explosion had occurred in the region and was precipitated by a bomb deep in the waters of the Mediterranean Sea just above or within the confines of the Leviathan Gas Works. Israel had been fortunate to find a vast source of gas and oil in this area and was about to drill for this valuable asset. Finding gas and oil would make Israel a competitor with the world market of energy sources and would certainly make Israel self reliant on any energy needs. The source of the explosion was unexplained, but the presence of radioactive materials in the region and its extension toward the coast of Israel raised the issue of sabotage-- and a nuclear attack on the sovereign State of Israel. Who perpetuated this dastardly act was still unclear. Surely, no one had come forward to claim responsibility for this action. Israel, in cooperation with the United States, continued to explore the Levantine Basin and adjoining areas. A question arose—how did the tsunami spread to the Tel Aviv area? It appeared to relate to the fact that the explosion had spread to adjacent gas drilling areas, and these were in the direction of Tel Aviv. Adding to the nature of the currents of the Mediterranean on that fateful evening, the thrust of the

M.S.PLATT THE LAST SUPPER

waves pursued a course towards Neve Tzedek and the adjoining coast of Tel Aviv.

An issue arose of whether a bomb could have caused a tsunami in the first place. Several authorities easily dismissed this notion. It was known that the United States in conjunction with New Zealand had conducted experiments in World War II. In these experiments, large loads of TNT were exploded on an island in the Pacific Ocean. However, the waves that were initiated were never of the intensity of a tsunami, and the concept was abandoned after the Hiroshima and Nagasaki bomb detonations resulted in the end of the war in 1945. Other investigators, however, raised the question whether detonations by a Nagasaki bomb, or worse, a high-energy hydrogen bomb could initiate a tsunami. When the tsunami events of 2004 in Indonesia and 2011 in Japan occurred, there were rumors that these were set off by hostile governments. But the facts did not support those wild notions. A detonation of a Nagasaki bomb would only yield the explosive force of 20 kilotons of TNT, and the energy derived from this explosion would be equal to a mere 6.3×10^{13} Joules of energy. Worse, if an explosion of a hydrogen bomb were considered, the explosive energy of 50 megatons of TNT and the energy equivalent of 2.1×10^{17} Joules would be achieved. Experts in these areas showed that these energy equivalents were infinitely inferior to the energy that caused the Indonesian and Japanese tsunamis. The earthquakes that initiated the tsunamis of these catastrophes were of the order of magnitude-9, yielding energy equivalents in the 20×10^{17} Joule range. Thus, any explosion of an atomic bomb was considered inferior and inadequate to initiate a tsunami.

Thus, experts in Israel and the U.S. government could not compel a theory that an atomic blast in the Levantine Basin could have initiated the Tel Aviv disaster. Besides, other questions arose. Why had not any party claimed the cause of the event? Why would an attack on the Levantine Basin take place at all? How much explosive energy would be necessary to cause a tsunami in the Levantine Basin? All of these questions raised the level of terror-consciousness and curiosity of all the nations in the Middle East as well as Western Europe and the United States since the auger of an attack on them would also be likely, and indeed, deadly. Thus, the investigations continued.

M.S.PLATT   THE LAST SUPPER

And for myself, I found that I was in the direst of circumstances as the days progressed. I continued to require more transfusions, and I was having infections of my skin, my lungs, and my blood stream. The doctors were concerned that I would expire. Unfortunately, my situation was unique. I was the only survivor of the tsunami and its preceding nuclear explosion near Neve Tzedek. A few other survivors who were two miles inland from the coast received much less radioactive exposure so that they were responding readily to supportive medical therapies.

My doctors surmised that I was subjected to a goodly amount of radiation. Therefore, I was experiencing acute radiation sickness. Radiation can affect the environment and humans from many sources. The most likely source in my situation was from something that was detonated in the Mediterranean Sea and had traveled in the water and mud. The explosion of a radioactive device emits gamma rays from radioactive chemical isotopes. Radiation exposure is measured by determining the amount of energy from gamma ionizing radiation in the air and absorbed by the body. The amount of energy emitted in the air is referred to as the 'roentgen', and the amount that is absorbed by the body is denominated as the 'radiation absorbed dose' or the 'rad'. Another unit of measurement, the 'rem', is the energy that is absorbed compared to the type of energy or type of tissue. It is the 'rad' corrected by a 'quantity factor'. For practicable purposes, in human analyses, the 'rem' is almost equivalent to the 'rad'. These terms are being replaced internationally by the terms 'the Gray' which is equivalent to 100 rads and 'the Sievert', equal to 100 rem. The doctors presumed that my exposure was probably in the range of 200 rads or 2.00 Gray. Higher doses of exposure can result in unconsciousness and death within a few days. The early symptoms of nausea, vomiting, and skin rash were consistent with a diagnosis of 200 rads. The bone marrow failure confirmed it. Certainly, the presence of radioactive materials on my skin and clothes supported that view.

To make matters worse, my neutrophil white count was approaching 500 cells per cu. mm. and my T cell count was down to 200 T cells per cu. mm. These levels were near lethal circumstances. Workers who expired during the Chernobyl disaster in the USSR in 1986 dropped to these levels. A few of those workers

M.S.PLATT THE LAST SUPPER

received bone marrow transfusions, abbreviated BMT, and survived. Thus, the staff at Rabin Memorial approached me about a BMT.

The purpose of a BMT is to replace the progenitor cells of the blood system, frequently referred to as the hematopoietic system. Bone marrow is obtained from a donor and transfused into the ill recipient. These are usually used in circumstances where a patient suffers from an advanced malignancy including those such as leukemia and lymphoma that are of the hematopoietic system. Bone marrow transplants are also given for hereditary bone marrow failures, inherited blood disorders, metabolic diseases, and aplastic anemia, a condition in which the bone marrow is destroyed by toxic materials. The ideal recipient, the patient, should be closely related to the donor. This is because if the donor and recipient are not closely related, the donor cells can attack the recipient's cells or, visa versa, the recipient can attack the donor cells. In either case, the BMT is rejected or, worse, the patient expires.

At times, a patient may have saved bone marrow cells or a blood product, and when needed, the specimen is transfused back into the patient. This type of BMT is referred to as an autologous BMT since 'auto' means 'self''. If an autologous specimen is not available, the patient must turn to another person and receive an allogeneic BMT from another donor. 'Allogeneic' means 'other'. Ideally, the other donor should be a close relative of the patient. A sibling is best. This is because the donor's genes are closely related or matched to the recipient. Special tests are performed to see if the donor and recipient are well matched. If a sibling is not available, an applicable match may be found in parents, children, or other relatives. Unfortunately, there may be no family members available for a match, and an unrelated person comes forward to donate. Matching these parties may be a difficult assignment, but unrelated parties can, at times, match. These are found through national bone marrow registries. Another source of a transplant is by use of umbilical cord blood. This is an allogeneic transplant, but newborn blood cells obtained from the placenta are immature and may match with the recipient.

   In my circumstance, I did not have a sibling or close relative to donate the material. My Israeli family members were lost at sea. The hospital was not able to easily find a closely matched donor. However, the Rabin Medical Center was the ideal place to obtain a transplant because this hospital was one of the leaders in the transplantation of organs and bone marrow in the country.

I was in a quandary. I shared this dilemma with Kristin. She had about given up on finding Neville or any of his remains and was considering returning to Britain.

"Kristin, maybe that is the best thing. You need to move forward with your life. You need to meet other people although you may find that notion unacceptable at this time of your life. I'm at my wits end. There is a potential donor, but the match is not the best. Dr. Bar Ilan is not sure if the transplant will take or if it will attack my body, and I will die of graft versus host disease, a condition where the donor's cells attack my cells, and I die."

"David. I have thought about your situation. Why not test my blood to see if there is any hope of a match? We have nothing to lose. Don't say another word. I will talk to Dr. Bar Ilan later and discuss it with him."

"Kristin, do you know what you are letting yourself in for?"

"David, don't be ridiculous. I am a geneticist and I know all about these things. As I said, I will talk to Dr. Bar Ilan, and don't try to dissuade me."

CHAPTER VI

True to her word, Kristin went to see Dr. Bar Ilan the following day.

"Hello, Dr. Bar Ilan. I think you know me. I am a friend of David Adams. I need to talk to you. He needs a bone marrow transplant. What can I do to help you? I would like to donate."

"Are you related to him?"

"No."

"Well, I see that you pregnant. We do not take donations from pregnant women. They may become anemic and compromise their pregnancy."

"I am aware of that," Kristin answered testily. "I am a geneticist at the University in London and work with medical people all the time."

"Oh. I see. What is your name again?"

Kristin Hudson. I am sure you are familiar with some of my papers in the literature."

M.S.PLATT   THE LAST SUPPER

Bar Ilan was caught off guard. He hesitated for a moment, and tried to recompose himself. He looked out the window and thought for several minutes. Then he turned to Kristin. "I—I do. Now that you mention it, I believe I have read your work. Rather impressed I must say. Then you are the wife of Neville Hudson, the famous archeologist, who went missing in the tsunami catastrophe."

"Indeed I am. Have you heard any word of his status?"

"No, I'm sorry to say. Still missing. But you realize then, that we cannot take any blood from you to help David. I feel so helpless for him. He is in need of multiple transfusions and is in dire straits because of the constant threat of infection."

"Yes, I know. Although I don't have access to his medical records, I know what is going on. I am due to deliver in a few weeks. You can use the umbilical and placental blood if it matches with David."

"Good point. We have had a difficult time getting a good match for him...even using a broad based registry of donors in Israel."

Kristin shifted her stance and approached Bar Ilan.

"Well, you and I know that placental blood has less restrictions for matching."

"Yes. I am aware of that, Dr. Hudson," he said somewhat defensively. "But as you know, we would need at least two donations of umbilical cord blood. One sample is insufficient. It doesn't give a sufficient number of cells to the recipient, and a take of the transfusion will not occur."

"True," Kristin responded gingerly. "But if you could now check the registries of umbilical cord blood, you may find a reasonable match for both my sample and that of another placenta that is in storage."

"Good thinking," Bar Ilan snapped back. Let me do some investigation and see if there are any closely matched stored umbilical blood samples in Israel. And, of course, we would need to test you and the umbilical blood sample of your child when it becomes available to see if it also matches with David. In the meantime, may I suggest that we test your blood to see if it is compatible? Then, if it is, we can check the newborn infant's blood sample."

"Then you will consider my suggestion?" Kristin pressed on.

"Of course. We have nothing to lose. And David's life depends on it. But time will be of the essence. I don't know how long he will hold out, and you won't deliver for about two weeks, I surmise, " looking at her abdomen.

"Yes, you are correct. I am at about 38 to 39 weeks gestation. I have been taking iron, folic acid and vitamins and a good diet to stay healthy, and I am in good condition. If necessary, your staff can perform a caesarian section and get the umbilical blood. If we are lucky, maybe I can deliver early and spontaneously. That, I am sure will be better. I have been under severe stress recently and labor may come on more rapidly."

"We would want you to be as healthy and comfortable as possible, Dr. Hudson. I know it is difficult with your husband Neville missing, but we both must pray that he is somewhere out there safe. In the meantime, I'll order some tests on you. By the way, may I call you Kristin instead of Dr. Hudson from now on."

"Of course," Kristin replied, smiling at him.

Kristin knew the risks and arduous challenges that she and David faced in this endeavor. Bone marrow transplantation had come a long way since it was first

M.S.PLATT   THE LAST SUPPER

entertained in the late 20th Century. At first, these transfusions were rejected, but blood bank specialists soon realized that tissue cells have proteins on their surfaces. These proteins or antigens identify the cell as a 'self" cell of the person. Anything foreign to the patient is recognized by the person's immune system. This system, present in all humans as well as animals, is designed to recognize anything that is foreign. If so, the body attacks the foreign cells and rejects them. It does so by stimulating the formation of antibodies and cells that help the body reject foreign material.

Antibodies are proteins that are made by the body to combine with the foreign cell. The joining of the foreign cell and antibody permits the patient to engulf and then digest the foreign material. The body also makes various cells that help it attack foreign material. Both of these activities are the function of a complicated and convoluted immune system. This notion works very well when a patient has an infection from a bacteria or virus. These are foreign to the patient so his or her immune system attacks the bacteria or virus and removes it from the body.

M.S.PLATT   THE LAST SUPPER

This doesn't work well when a blood transfusion or bone marrow transplant is injected into the body. The blood transfusion or bone marrow transplant may be viewed as foreign material when injected into the patient. In regard to blood transfusions, humans have four blood types. Each is related to a protein or antigen on the surface of the red blood cells. Some people have antibodies in their blood, and these can react against antigens on the surfaces of the red cells. For instance, some people have O type blood. These red cells have very few antigens on their surface and can donate blood to many people. These are called 'universal donors' because the recipient's antibodies do not attack the O cells. Other people have A, B, or AB blood types. These people cannot receive blood from everyone, but need to be tested first to see if they are compatible with the donated blood. People with AB type blood have no anti A or anti B antibodies in their blood so they can receive types O, A, B, or AB blood. They are referred to as 'universal recipients'.

One also needs to check a patient's Rh status. Serum or plasma, the clear fluid of a person's blood, is tested against anti Rh antibodies obtained from another source. If the cells clot, the patient is Rh positive.

A third test that must be done is called a 'cross match'. In this case, the patient's serum is tested against a variety of red blood cells from other patients. If these clot when tested, the recipient patient may have 'irregular antibodies' in their serum, and these would react with any donated blood. These 'irregular antibodies' need to be identified so that any red cell that contains an antigen for that antibody will not be donated because the donation will cause a reaction in the recipient's blood after the donation.

The major breakthrough in tissue, organ and bone marrow transfusions was the identification of tissue antigens on the surfaces of all the cells in humans. There are over 100 different antigens or proteins on the surface of a person's cells, but about 6 to 10 are most important in tissue transplantation.

Every person inherits half of these antigen sites from each parent according to genetic inheritance patterns. Antibodies are available to test for the presence of these antigens on the tissue cell surfaces. Fortunately, a person's white blood cells or leucocytes can be used for these tests so the test is called a 'human leucocyte antigen' test or HLA test. The human leucocyte antigen system is based on genes that are encoded on these cells. These involve the major histocompatibility complex (MHC) proteins in humans. These surface proteins or antigens are responsible for the regulation of the immune system in humans so identification of these sites is necessary to make sure that the immune system does not reject a transplant.

Kristin knew that this system was intricate. There are several MCH classes. Class I cells are found at A, B, and C sites within white cells. If a virus infects a cell, the Class I HLA system brings the fragments of the virus to the surface of the cell so that the cell can be destroyed by the patient's immune system. The Class II HLA system works differently. It presents antigens from outside the cell to T cell lymphocytes that help destroy the cell that contains the virus or bacteria.

Kristin knew that all these systems were complicated, but she knew how they worked. These pathways allowed bone marrow transplants to be accepted by very ill patients.

Thus, Kristin knew that unless her HLA tissue cell types closely matched that of David's, her bone marrow cells would be attacked by his immune system, and the transplant would die. In the alternative, Kristin's immune cells that were transfused into David could attack his cells, and he would get a graft versus host reaction or GVH disease. In either case, a war would ensue between Kristin's and David's bone marrow cells and immune systems. The outcome could be the acceptance of the graft, rejection of the graft, or a constant battle between Kristin and David's immune systems. In the latter two circumstances, the undesirable end result would be transplant failure, infection and death.

As a medical geneticist and person deeply active in the care of these patients in London, Kristin was aware that medications are given to transplant patients prior to and after the transplant. These medications modulate and tone down the immune system of the recipient so that his or her immune system does not attack the donor cells too vigorously. These medications are also given after the transplant so that the donor's transplanted cells do not attack the recipient and initiate GVH disease.

Thus, the challenge in the transplant process is to have a good match between recipient and donor and to judiciously use immune system modulating drugs. Transplant physicians identify a minimum of six HLA antigen sites, but many test up to ten sites. The objective is to obtain a 6/6 match or a 10/10 match on 6 point or 10 point scales; that is, 6 of the antigen sites of the donor match 6 sites of the recipient or 10 sites match 10 sites. Sibling matches offer the best odds; 25 % of these yield a 6/6 match. A parent or child is next best; but only 12% have a perfect match. Unrelated donors considerably decrease the chance of a perfect match. Unfortunately, 70 % of patients who need a transplant do not have a donor in their family. David was clearly within this category.

Many institutions now test for 10 HLA markers: two at A sites, two at B, two at C, two at the DRB 1, and two at the DQ site. Because David and Kristin were not related, the match would require a 6/8 match, at least. However, since David was to receive cord blood in the transplant, he was more fortunate. Cord blood cells are less mature and only 4 out of 6 markers at A, B, and DRB 1 sites are necessary. In addition, he was receiving cells from a Caucasian male. Ultrasound studies in Britain had shown that Kristin's baby was a male, and male donor transplants tend to cause less rejection.

David was also fortunate that the Rabin Center was able to perform high resolution HLA typing by using genetic specific markers so that it was possible to get a better match.

Of course, these ideal circumstances rested on two important facts. One was that the umbilical cord transplant from Kristin's baby would yield a large number of cells, and the other was that another umbilical cord specimen would be readily available and that it too would offer a very good match and be fresh enough to yield a sufficient number of cells.

The transplant staff at Rabin realized that umbilical cord blood transplants took longer to engraft, but that was another risk that they would have to undertake.

So Kristin underwent the procedures for testing her tissue and blood types. Admittedly, her HLA cell type would be only one half of the baby's type since its genetic code would constitute half from Kristin and half from her husband Neville, but if Kristin's HLA match was close, the hope for a successful transplant still existed. Only the HLA match of the newborn's cord blood and David would clarify the issue and set the hope for a successful transplant.

   Kristin's HLA tests were performed on samples taken from her blood and mouth swabs since genetic findings could be obtained from both sources. She also underwent numerous tests to rule-out any virus infections, for these could severely compromise the transplantation process.

Kristin was fortunate that she could donate her newborn's umbilical and placental blood because it saved her from undergoing other methods of bone marrow acquisition. Historically, donors would be subject to needle biopsies of their hipbones where marrow samples would be collected. This was a painful process. Later on, investigators learned that peripheral blood, blood collected from a donor's veins, would be rich in bone marrow progenitor/stem cells. Blood would be collected using a sophisticated instrument such that the white cells and stem cells would be separated by various means and the unused red cells and platelets returned to the donor. This process, called apheresis, made collection easier, but the donor's cells still needed to be matched with the recipient's tissue cells. It also needed to be collected aseptically so that neither the donor nor recipient would acquire any infection during the collection process. In order to increase the yield of white and stem cells, donors were, at times, required to inject cell growth medications daily. The collection process took 3 to 4 hours over a 2 or more day period until a sufficient number of cells were collected.

But Kristin did not need to undergo these procedures. She only needed to have a healthy baby boy who could donate his umbilical and placental blood. The placenta or afterbirth is that organ that develops during pregnancy. It takes oxygen and nutrients from the mother's blood and delivers them through the umbilical cord to the growing fetus. Conversely, waste products from the fetus travel through the cord to the placenta where they are transported to the mother's blood and eliminated by her.

When Kristin's baby would be delivered, the umbilical cord would be clamped and cut. Her newborn would no longer need the placental blood. The placenta would be expelled from her uterus after the birth of the baby. The stem cell rich blood would be collected aseptically from the umbilical blood vessels. These cells would then mature into all the common types of blood cells when transfused into the David.

Kristin subjected herself to all the blood tests and waited for the results, hoping that a reasonable match with David could be found.

While Kristin waited for the results, the government of Israel pursued the investigation of the alleged tsunami.

CHAPTER VII

The Israeli government now faced four disturbing facts: 1) an atomic device had been detonated a mere 90 miles from its western shore, 2) the device initiated waves of water that destroyed the Mediterranean coastal area of Tel Aviv and penetrated two miles inland, 3) their once valuable Leviathan gas fields were now utterly destroyed, and 4) the perpetuator or perpetuators of this effrontery were not yet identified. Israeli citizens did not consider these circumstances benignly; they demanded vigorous investigation, ascertainment of hard factual evidence, and an aggressive response without delay. The challenges fell on the ministries of defense and interior as well as the secret service agency of Israel, the Mossad. Agents rapidly dispersed into the fields of destruction and radiation danger seeking that evidence.

For Israel, the art of war had seemingly changed by the 21st Century. Nations no longer performed aggressive acts against each other and then formally declared a state of war. Instead, groups within nations would claim that outside parties with advanced cultures or economic agendas were acting as oppressors of their less fortunate minorities. And these groups, rather than nations as a whole, would claim that they had a duty to protect the rights of the oppressed. Partisans and defenders of the alleged oppressed people would vow to seek justice by performing acts of terror and destruction against any opponent, race or entity that allegedly caused the presumed injustice. Formally declared wars had now become a subliminal phenomenon, but the atrocities of war would remain unabated; and mistrust, hostile actions, and conflict would still become dominant themes. The will of one nation would confront the will of another, not as declared war, but as hostile and destabilizing effronteries against groups in another nation or—if necessary—within the nation itself. The parties of these actions no longer acted as nation-states or specific entities but as invisible groups who sought their own agendas, their own notions of 'righteous justice'. If anarchy or chaos uprooted the legal and moral sinews of another nation, so be it. The agendas of these complaining groups were primary even though their actions disrupted civil dialogue and the will of the majority.

Thus, the Arab of Palestine would 'rightfully' oppose and confront the Jew of Israel, notwithstanding the fact that the populations of Palestine and Israel were not formally at war. The Shi'ite of Yemen would confront the Sunni of Yemen. Similarly, armed bandits of central African states would attack, mutilate, and destroy whole communities within their own national boundaries, always claiming to seek personal justice or designs of their own making. And the Western nations of Europe as well as the United States would be reminded that they were guilty *de novo* of transgressions that initiated the injustices.

Thus, Israel found itself alone and abandoned. Its national sovereignty had been compromised. Rogue parties within rogue states had attacked it, and its very life was at stake. Israel's investigative forces reached out to all areas of the world seeking information and help from any nation that would appear friendly to it.

The nature of the atomic explosion and its relationship to the alleged tsunami was addressed first. Authorities in the United States disparaged the notion that an atomic blast could initiate a tsunami. They pointed out that experiments in the Pacific during World War II were unsuccessful and that the energy of any atomic devise would be insufficient to match the energy of a 9.0-magnitude earthquake. However, the Israeli investigators pressed the issue and explored the floor of the Mediterranean at the Leviathan gas-drilling site. The Mossad was amazed to find that remnants of a 'bathyscaphe' were found floating in the waters of the Mediterranean. The history of a 'bathyscaphe' or 'floating ship' was known since 1960. It was the year

M.S.PLATT   THE LAST SUPPER

Piccard and Walsh used such an instrument. They descended to the lowest
point of the Pacific Ocean, 36,000 feet, at the Mariana Trench near Guam. Their instrument had a cabin for two, a gasoline filled float, and iron shot held in place by an electromagnet. The latter was used as ballast to descend to the ocean floor. The iron shot would be discharged so that the ship could ascend. In 2009, a hybrid unmanned autonomous underwater vehicle, named the Nereus, became available. It could operate tethered to a thin optic fiber cable or untethered and operate as a free-swimming vehicle and survey the ocean floor. If tethered, it was attached to a slender glass fiber cable that was wound in two small canisters that played out for 5 miles as the ship descended. The Nereus weighed 3 tons in air and was about 14 feet long and 8 feet wide. Approximately 2,000 lithium-ion batteries provided its power. It was built with about 800 ceramic hollow spheres that would handle the intense pressure, sometimes 1,000 times atmospheric pressure, as it descended. It had a lightweight robotic manipulator arm to collect samples and could be operated by pilots from an adjacent ship. Unfortunately,

the Nereus unexpectedly disappeared in 2014 while on a mission and was never found again. Interestingly, the Israeli divers were able to retrieve fragments of ceramic debris on the Mediterranean seabed at the site of the explosion.

In addition, the maximum sources of radiation did indeed arise at the site of the Levantine Basin area. When Israeli naval vessels and deep-sea explorative instruments were dropped into the area of severe damage, the Israeli investigators found that a nuclear explosion had destroyed the drilling apparatus at the Leviathan and its adjacent wells. But the major finding was that a massive landslide had ensued at the floor-bed of the sea. Tons of rock and wet sediment had dropped into the deep caverns that at one time contained the gas and oil below the sea floor. Calculations by Israeli engineers led them to believe that the detonation of a small nuclear devise was only part of the energy that affected the area. The Leviathan and Tamar gas field caverns were somehow connected, and the nuclear explosion caused the gas and oil in both fields to ignite and explode simultaneously. This singular event caused an implosion into the caverns such that gigantic waves, similar to those of the ancient landslides in the Mt. Etna earthquakes 8000 years previously, likely ensued. A bomb of the Nagasaki category with a mere 20 kilotons of TNT might not be adequate to initiate tsunami waves as espoused by the American authorities, but the explosion of the gas and oil deposits in the wells was another matter. The Leviathan gas field contained 22×10^{12} cubic feet of gas. Each cubic foot of gas had the energy of 1.055×10^6 Joules. When ignited and exploded, the gas field would yield a maximum of 23.21×10^{18} Joules. Although a Nagasaki type bomb would only yield 8.4×10^{13} Joules of energy, its explosion plus the vast explosion of a major portion of the gas field would yield more than enough. It would be greater than the energy of a 9.0-magnitude earthquake—that of 20×10^{17} Joules. If one then also added the energy acquired by the deep seabed landslide, a tsunami similar to one acquired in the magnitude-9.0 earthquake in Japan could easily produce similar tsunami waves only 80-90 miles away. The Japanese earthquake epicenter was but 80 miles from the Japanese coast, and it penetrated 6 miles inland! The lower magnitude of 7.0 in the Israeli explosion registered on seismographs could be explained by a combination of a smaller bomb, explosions of the gas and oil wells, the massive underwater landslide, and the absence of an earthquake.

The next enigma that demanded explanation was: Why were the gas fields destroyed and who could have perpetuated this egregious act? This question was less easy to answer since no one party had made a claim to the sabotage. However, several parties of interest soon came to mind:

1) Egypt had recently found a gas field larger than the Leviathan. Did it wish to remove any competitor?
2) Hezbollah had threatened to attack the Israeli gas fields. Where would it get the bomb?
3) Cyprus and Turkey had claimed the Mediterranean as sites for exploration.
4) Iran would stand to lose large amounts of income if Israel had now become a producer of gas and oil. Iran certainly knew how to make nuclear materials. Did it produce a bomb?

5) Saudi Arabia would also lose income from Israeli competition. It also feared that Iran might produce a nuclear bomb. Did its conservative Sunni constituents choose to pre-empt Israel and test its own bomb prior to using it against Iran?
6) Could the rogues of North Korea be seeking to disrupt the Middle East because of some disagreement with the Arabs? Had the Arabs previously purchased nuclear equipment from them and not paid the bill?

Unfortunately, these questions could not be answered. Thus, Israel, alone and abandoned, turned to the United States and the United Nations for help.

Israel's prime minister contacted his ambassador to the United Nations to register complaints against this intrusion and act of war against it. Its ambassador conveyed the complaints to the United Nations. In response, the United Nations advised, after some considerable delay, that:

a) The UN would refer the complaints to appropriate committees within the UN hierarchy.

b) The UN was exceedingly troubled by the conflicts in the Middle East, especially between Israel and Palestine.
c) The UN had advised Israel on innumerable occasions about the atrocities and oppressions committed by Israel against Palestine.
d) In fact, since 2003, it had sent to Israel at least 232 resolutions dealing with these incidents.
e) Israel should respond to these serious incidents and come forward with a constructive resolution that is fair to the Palestinian people.

The Israeli ambassador to the UN was much discomforted by this reply but carefully drafted a response to his prime minister explaining that he had planned to give a talk in the UN chambers but was unsure if the UN would assist Israel.

Israel's prime minister astutely realized that the best ally for his nation was the United States so he telephoned the President of the United States.

"Hello, Mr. President. You know what has happened here on our west coast. In fact, we now know that a small nuclear device sabotaged our oil and gas fields, and there is radiation fallout spreading eastward over our land. I have appreciated all the help you have given my scientists in ascertaining these facts, but you need to help us in a more proactive fashion."

The U.S. president conveyed to the prime minister the concern of the United States and advised Israel that the matter was and would be taken up by various committees of Congress.

Members of the president's cabinet expressed concern about the nuclear radiation and its fallout, but were reluctant to send U.S. military forces at this time because:

    a) There was a recession in the U.S., and funds were not readily available.
    b) The U. S. debt was now in excess of $20 trillion and growing because of necessary domestic expenditures in light of the economic crisis.
    c) The cabinet officers would contact the Congress and gain their responses.

The U. S. Congressional committees were quite interested in the request by the Israeli prime minister. Some committees advised the president that the U.S.

had already given Israel extensive military aid and was constrained now because of the world economic crisis and depression. The domestic situation did not help. Several committee chairpersons from congressional districts with large Jewish populations felt compelled to offer legislation to offer more military aid, but their motions never passed muster with sufficient committee votes. The Congress appeared to be at a standstill in aggressively dealing with the 'Israeli-Problem' as it was now denominated. Certainly, other countries in the world were having similar problems so the best that any nation could offer Israel was concern and a desire to find out more information before anyone would act. After all, the culprit of this attack was still not identified. The reasons for the attack had not been clearly delineated. Therefore, many nations, including the United States declared a 'watch-and-wait' attitude to the Israeli issue. As many would declare, "Time will tell what is going on, and then we will act responsibly. One cannot act responsibly if one does not have all the facts."

CHAPTER VIII

David's situation, just as the one in Israel, did not improve. He remained in reverse isolation and at risk for infection. His anemia, blood counts and platelet counts continued to falter. Kristin would visit him almost daily but could not touch him, comfort him, or speak closely with him. She was now becoming fully 'rotund' with her pregnancy, waiting for the hopeful birth date.

Weeks passed. The only fruitful signs were from the hematology, blood, and genetics laboratories. Kristin's blood and genetic tests showed that she was a 5/6 match with David. At first, that was odd since a 6/6 match of an allogeneic sample had an odds ratio of 1:100,000. The genetic tests also revealed that her blood had some unusual characteristics of Jewish blood, particularly odd since she was an Anglo-Saxon, red headed woman with a family history of British ancestry. So what were some of these interesting findings?

Initial studies evaluated seven blood groups and twelve red blood cell enzymes. These showed high frequencies of some of the blood types that had been noted in other studies involving Levant and European Jews. Several rare variants of proteins were found in Kristin's serum, and these matched those seen in these same populations. The research staffs at Rabin Medical Center decided to carry their studies further but waited until Kristin delivered her baby boy.

Kristin took great delight in her pregnancy. It was a symbol of her firm bonding with Neville, her now lost husband. It was a symbol of the continuity of life through her and Neville.

She was also uplifted when she went to the Tel Aviv branch of Bank Hapoalim. It had not been damaged by the tsunami. Kristin needed funds transferred from her London bank to Israel. As she approached the manager of the bank, he stood up and greeted her. "Shalom. May I help you?"

"Good afternoon. I am Doctor Kristin Hudson from Great Britain. I have an account with a London bank, and you have an international service. I need funds transferred to this bank. I don't know how long I will stay in Israel. As you can see, I am pregnant and due to deliver soon. My husband is missing in the tsunami, and I have no one to turn to. Can you help me?"

"Of course," he replied sadly. "Write down the details of your bank in London on this form, and I shall get you the funds wired here. Who is your husband?"

"Doctor Neville Hudson. He was on an archeological expedition in the Middle East. I am sure you've heard of him."

"Neville Hudson? He was a friend of David Adams. Oh, my God! David is a friend of some of my family members who are also missing. They were attending a Seder on Passover when the tragedy occurred. Then you know David, I presume? He is a patient at Rabin Medical Center."

"I know him very well by now. I have visited him at the hospital, and I know he is very ill. We were separately registered at a hotel in Petah Tikva when he became ill and was admitted to the hospital. I need these funds as soon as possible. I have bills to pay. I need to find a place to stay other than the hotel."

"Doctor Hudson. I am Rueben Leibowitz. Shlomo was my cousin. I will put 1000 Israeli shekels into an account in your name that I will set up immediately. When your funds arrive from London, I will make any necessary adjustments. If you know David, you are like family to me. Doctor Hudson, you can stay with my wife and me. Check out of the hotel. Wait. Let me call my wife."

He turned briskly to his left, grasped a phone, and dialed a number. "Rivka. Rivka. This is Rueben at the bank. I have a most interesting and sad thing I need to share with you. I have a woman from London who is married to Neville Hudson who was visiting at the Seder at Abram's house with Shlomo and Leah when the tragedy struck. She is almost due to deliver a baby, and she needs a place to stay…I know you would want to help. Come…Come to the bank and take her home with you. She is staying at the hotel in Petah Tikva near the hospital. Since we live in the same neighborhood as the hospital, it should not be a problem to move her in with us."

"Mr. Leibowitz," Kristin interrupted. "Wait. You don't have to go through all this trouble. I am sure I can survive."

M.S.PLATT   THE LAST SUPPER

"Doctor Hudson. I won't think twice about this. You are almost like family. Any friend of David and Shlomo and Leah, may they rest in peace, is like family to us. We wish that they were still alive, but Rivka and I are giving up hope. My wife will be here in about an hour. Please… Please take a seat in my office. I will get you a cup of tea and you can rest until my wife comes to take you to our home. In the meantime, I will handle your accounts." He disappeared into another room and beckoned Kristin to enter his office, brewed some tea, served her and disappeared again.

Rueben and Rivka became family to Kristin and arranged for her to find an apartment close to them and to offer support during the latter part of her pregnancy. They even sent notes to David in the hospital to wish him better health during his travails.

Kristin was now close to term, and she began early labor in the middle of the night. Her friends took her to the medical center, and the staff prepared her, the baby and the important umbilical blood for processing.

Labor for this first pregnancy mother lasted its usual 20 hours, but a healthy 6 pound, 3 ounce boy was born, free of defects, healthy in heart and lungs, and as spirited and sprite as Kristin always remembered Neville. Her newly adopted family members were close at hand when the baby was born, and when it was time to return her to the new apartment.

The major challenge now was preparing me for the umbilical cord blood transfusion. The umbilical cord blood also needed to be treated so that it would not injure me when injected. There was always fear that a graft versus host reaction would ensue and that the transfused cells would attack me in an aggressive immunological manner and kill me.

The first challenge was that of reducing the activity of my immune system. Generally, bone marrow recipients receive ablative treatment with high dose chemotherapy and radiation. This treatment, however, is used mainly in patients with cancer cells in their bone marrow, and the treatment is designed to eradicate these cells. In my case, I did not have a malignancy in my body. I was suffering from the toxic irradiation effect on my native bone marrow. Thus, a less aggressive approach was used. This procedure, called reduced intensity treatment, consisted of lower doses of chemotherapy before receiving the transplant. Then my immune system would quiet-down and not attack the donated bone marrow cells but allow these cells to grow unabated.

Another approach would be to treat the umbilical blood so as to deplete the T cells in the donor sample. The remaining cells including the blood forming stem cells would then be infused. New T cells might form from the donated blood stem cells, but these would be less likely to cause the graft versus host disease (GVHD).

There was another issue in my case. One unit of umbilical blood from Kristin's baby would not contain a sufficient number of stem cells to repopulate my marrow. I needed another donation of umbilical cord blood. Fortunately, an Arab woman had given birth to a healthy infant the day before. This woman had another child who was seriously injured in an auto accident previously, but that child survived when aggressively treated by the medical and surgical staffs at Rabin. In appreciation of the staff's efforts, she elected to donate her next child's umbilical blood. This donation was significant since donations of umbilical blood must be voluntary, never coerced or purchased. Her benevolent action was symbolic of a hopeful growing relationship with the Arab and Jewish communities. Fortunately, there was a 4/6 match for this donation, and although this match from an allogeneic donor would be insufficient from the general population, umbilical cord blood, consisting of less mature cells, would have a better odds ratio of accepting the graft and a lower odds ratio of developing GVHD. I was also fortunate that the donations were A+, my same blood type, so that blood type incompatibilities would not arise.

  With great anticipation, the medical staffs collected and treated the donated samples, and injected them through a large bore needle in my arm. The stem cells would then become resident in my marrow after circulating within my blood stream. Hopefully, they would engraft and grow. Time would clarify the issue whether the transfusion would work to correct my marrow failure or not. In the meantime, close observation for the appearance of early signs of GVHD would be a challenge on a daily basis, and I was treated prophylactically with various medications such as cyclosporine, tacrolimus, and antithymocyte globulin medications that inhibit T cell function and, therefore, reduce GVHD.

M.S.PLATT THE LAST SUPPER

I was subjected to daily blood tests. On the second week after my transplant, I began to experience a red rash on my chest, mild jaundice in my eyes and mild diarrhea. There was concern that I was having early acute GVHD and prednisolone, a corticosteroid, was added to my regimen.

I was happy to hear that Kristin and her new son were settled in the new apartment near Rivka and Rueben, and that they were helping her make life tolerable.

A week later, I was surprised to see Kristin, full in gown, gloves and attire facing me through a window in the room. A nurse, also fully attired, allowed Kristin to enter my reverse isolation room. Kristin slowly approached me, pulled her crucifix from her necklace and cleansed it with an antiseptic solution. She then touched the crucifix to my surgical gown at my chest and whispered, "David, I pray that the LORD heal you, and protect you. May He turn to you and make you well again." A few misty tears could be seen at the top of her surgical mask, and she turned spritely around and left the room.

M.S.PLATT   THE LAST SUPPER

Three weeks into my post transplant status the medical team advised me that my transplant had shown signs of early engraftment. New cells were starting to show up in my blood.

Kristin would visit me frequently and see me through the isolation-protected window. She would send me notes, conveyed to me by the nurse, telling me how she was surviving, how baby Neville was growing, and showing me photos of him through the window.

When Baby Neville was a month old, Kristin arranged for a Christening ceremony at an Anglican Church in Jerusalem. Rueben and Rivka agreed to accompany her even though they were Jewish. Although they could not serve as godparents, they did advise the priest at the ceremony that they would help Kristin raise Neville to become a good, upright Christian in the years ahead.

The genetics staff at Rabin Medical Center became familiar with Kristin's work in Britain, and she began to attend genetic conferences. In time, she was offered a position in the genetics department, and she decided to further explore the significance of her blood tests, for these presented a challenge as well as an enigma as to their implications.

M.S.PLATT   THE LAST SUPPER

CHAPTER IX

Kristin knew that her red blood cell enzymes, white blood cells, and serum proteins had markers that were commonly seen in Jewish populations. But this knowledge enticed her to move forward, to seek more information. To do this, she would use studies that were as sophisticated as those used in tissue typing. The genetic analysis of blood and DNA had moved vastly forward in the past 30 years, and these studies were now available so that she could clarify the issue of her alleged Jewish background. She was now a genetics section supervisor at Rabin Medical Center and could pursue these tests without any administrative obstruction or financial restrictions.

Kristin knew that living cells replace or reproduce themselves. In human beings, the instruction for this process is maintained in the nucleus of each cell. Humans contain eukaryotic cells; that is, each cell has a membrane-lined nucleus. Each human cell nucleus contains 23-paired chromosomes, a total of 46. Two pairs are sex chromosomes. These are designated X and Y. Each female of the human species has a paired XX sex chromosome component, and these determine the female characteristics of the fetus. Each male has a XY sex component. The Y chromosome instructs the growing fetus to develop male secondary sexual characteristics throughout life. The other 22 pairs are designated the autosome chromosomes. These contain the genetic instructions for the development of all the other non-sexual components of the fetus. Each chromosome contains the instructions in a single piece of coiled double strand of DNA containing many genes, regulatory elements and other non-coding DNA. Compaction of the chromosome occurs during cell division into four arm or two arm structures. Chromosome recombination that occurs during cell division or sexual reproduction plays a significant role in genetic diversity.

How does DNA operate in this scenario? The packed nuclear DNA within a cell governs every human, animal or plant reproductive cycle. In sexual reproduction, these organisms inherit half of their nuclear DNA from the male parent and half from the female parent. An organism's complete set of nuclear DNA is called its genome. In addition to the DNA located in the nucleus,

M.S.PLATT   THE LAST SUPPER

humans and other complex organisms have a small amount of DNA in other cell structures known as mitochondria. The mitochondria generate the energy that the cell needs to function properly. Organisms inherit all their mitochondrial DNA from the female parent because only eggs cells, not sperm cells, keep their mitochondria during fertilization.

When a cell prepares to divide, the DNA coiled helix splits down the middle and becomes two strands. The single strands serve as templates for building two new double stranded DNA molecules— each a replica of the original molecule. During sexual reproduction, each single strand is carried by the male sex cell to join with the female sex cell and form the full complement of 46 chromosomes.

The study of DNA and chromosomes has undergone a series of sophisticated developments. In 1956, the true number of human chromosomes was finally determined to be 46. In the mid 20th Century, it was found in metaphase, an early stage of cell division, that the chromatin of chromosomal material became more condensed and could be stained by vital dyes. Photographs of these metaphase stages of cell division allowed researchers to study all 46 of the chromosomes. When these were photographed, a person's karyotype could be analyzed. Aberrations in the number and size of the various chromosomes led to a rapid advance in the knowledge of chromosomal diseases. An extra copy of chromosome 21 characterized Down syndrome. These patients exhibited slanting yes, decreased muscle tone, heart defects and mild to moderate developmental disabilities. Cancers such as acute lymphocytic leukemia and the Philadelphia chromosome in chronic myeloid leukemia were soon discovered to have other chromosome abnormalities.

Remarkable progress in individual gene analysis also moved forward in the late 20th and early 21st Centuries. DNA microarray analysis introduced in the 1980's utilized a collection of microscopic DNA spots attached to a solid surface in order to measure the expression levels of a large number of genes simultaneously or to genotype regions of a gene.

Whole genome sequencing determined the complete DNA sequence of a patient's genome in one test, and analyzed both the nuclear and mitochondrial DNA. Whole exome sequencing was introduced as a technique for sequencing all the expressed genes in a genome by first selecting only the portion of DNA that encodes proteins. This test was used to identify common diseases without the high cost of whole genome sequencing.

Almost any biological sample containing a full copy of DNA could now be used. This included saliva, epithelial cells from the mouth or body, bone marrow, or hair follicle cells. Analyses from a patient now permitted geneticists to determine if a patient had any genetic mutations, specific diseases or have a cancer cell of interest. One could also determine if a patient lacked the ability to utilize or metabolize a drug. Geneticists could determine if there were any differences between cell samples and advise forensic scientists if the DNA of an accused was the true sample found in a rape victim.

DNA is formed by chemical building blocks called nucleotides. These are made up of three parts: a phosphate group, a sugar group, and one of four types of nitrogen compounds called nucleotide bases. The four types of these bases are adenine (A), thymine (T), guanine (G), and cytosine (C). The order or sequence of these bases in the DNA molecule determines what genetic instruction will be given. When these are transferred to a cell, groups of three nucleotide bases, called codons, are translated by the cell machinery and direct the formation of all the 24 essential amino acids found in humans. For example, a codon with the genetic code TTC will form the amino acid phenylalanine. The codon GTT will make valine. In concert, all the amino acids direct a human life's processes. One could picture the codon process as Natures or God's way of creating a symphony composed of multiple musical notes, and the entire symphony—the DNA—would create a symphony of one's life.

Another form of genetic analysis, SNP genotyping, permitted the measurement of single nucleotide polymorphisms or genetic variations of the nucleotides. SNP's are conserved during evolution so SNP microarrays on beads allowed geneticists to study hundreds of thousands of individuals for genome-wide variations across vast geographic areas including those of the Jewish Diaspora communities in North Africa and Europe. In 2010, it was shown that Jews had a genetic closeness in communities as diverse as those from Europe, North Africa and the Ottoman Empire. Thus,

M.S.PLATT   THE LAST SUPPER

Ashkenazim from Eastern Europe and Sephardim Jews from the Middle East, North Africa and Spain were related. These studies refuted the suggestion by others that Jews had no common origin but were the composite result of people who converted to Judaism at various times. Instead, these recent studies showed that Jewish communities from Europe, the Middle East, and the Caucasian regions had substantial genetically shared ancestry that traced back to the Levant. In fact, the shared genetic information suggested that members of any Jewish community could be as closely related as fourth or fifth cousins in a large population, a finding that is ten times higher than any relationship between two other people chosen at random in New York City.

One group of investigators even developed a way of timing the demographic events from the genetic elements of deported Jewish communities and showed that Iraqi and Iranian Jews separated from other Jewish communities about 2,500 years ago, reflecting the time when the First Temple was destroyed in 586 BCE. These were the Jews of the northern kingdom, the ten lost tribes, who were deported to Iraq and Iran/Persia. All these data supported the findings by Neville Hudson when he discovered the Esther Tablets in the Zagros Mountains near Shushan.

It was this information that spurned Kristin to pursue the nature of her genetic material. And this she did. Indeed, she found that her genetic material was similar to the Jewish populations of North Africa of the Levant as well that of Central Europe.

An explanation was therefore in order, and Kristin, scientist to the core, elected to pursue this enigma. She pressed the issue with various government sources in Britain where her family lived. There were, unfortunately, few live family remaining after three generations and the devastating destruction in Britain during World War II, but she was amazed to learn that a child was brought to Britain in 1938 and that this child was adopted by a family in Britain. The child—Sophie Mueller—was born in 1932 in Nuremberg, Germany and sent to Coventry, England in 1938. She was adopted by a Miller family in Coventry, and raised as a Christian in the Anglican Church. She married at age 23 years in 1955 and had a child—named Anna Boyle -- in 1957. Anna was also raised as an Anglican, married in 1979 at the age of 22 years and had a child—Kristin –- in 1981.

M.S.PLATT   THE LAST SUPPER

Kristin married a Neville Hudson in 2015. At the time, she was 34 years old. This person is the same Kristin Hudson, now in Israel, and the mother of Neville Hudson, Jr.

Obviously, the missing link was this Sophie Mueller who immigrated to Britain and was adopted in 1938. Getting German data would not be easy. World War II devastated Nazi Germany and Kristin did not know where to look for data in Germany. Should she try West Germany? Should she try East Germany under the influence of the Communist Regimes?

Fortunately, Kristin obtained the adoption papers from Coventry. Local governments were now allowing adopted children to find out the names of their blood parents and relatives. The Mueller name would be a valuable clue. The adoption papers indicated that Sophie Mueller was sent to Britain by a Mueller aunt, living in Nuremberg, Germany in 1938. Kristin was not sure if she would find any relatives in Nuremberg, but she relied on the organized behavior of the Teutonic people. She implored authorities in Nuremberg to search the records of 1938 in regard to a deportation of a child by the name of Mueller from Nuremberg to a

M.S.PLATT   THE LAST SUPPER

family in Britain by the name of Miller. She also increased her search for information about the 1938 adoption in Coventry. Numerous telephone calls, letters of inquiry and e-mails to government authorities in both localities resulted in few responses, but Kristin eventually received a parcel two months later. It was from Nuremberg. Anxiously, and with trembling fingers, she opened the packet. A multiple-paged report was enclosed, and it shed the following information:

A Sophie Mueller was given permission to immigrate to Coventry, England in November 1938 following the death of her father Heinrich Mueller and mother Lilli Mueller during the Kristallnacht events of 9-10 November 1938. Her father Heinrich had been a soldier in the German army in World War I and was wounded but served honorably and returned to civilian life in the Weimar Republic following the war. Heinrich was of Jewish blood and had married a Lutheran woman, Lilli Albrecht, in the 1920's. They had a female child— Sophie Mueller-- in 1932. Heinrich and Lilli owned a store in Nuremberg. It was designed to offer medical equipment to doctors but now had fallen on hard times and sold small trinkets to tourists. Kristallnacht was the

M.S.PLATT   THE LAST SUPPER

name given to that night of November 1938 because of the presence of shards of broken glass that littered the streets after Jewish-owned stores, buildings and synagogues had their windows smashed by SA paramilitary forces and German civilians following the assassination of the German diplomat Ernest von Roth by Herschel Grynszpan, a German-born Polish Jew living in Paris. The death of Heinrich and Lilli following the tumult of Kristallnacht left their child Sophie an orphan. Although Heinrich was Jewish, his wife was Lutheran and their child was born of a Christian mother.

The Nazis took control of Germany in 1933. In Nuremberg, in 1935, the Nazis announced new laws that institutionalized many of the racial theories prevalent in Nazi ideology. The laws excluded German Jews from Reich citizenship and prohibited them marrying or having sexual relations with persons of German or related blood. Other laws deprived Jews of most political rights and disenfranchised them. Jewish doctors, lawyers and civil servants could not practice their professions and were reduced to meager life styles and employment. The Nuremberg Laws did not define a Jew as someone with a particular religious belief.

Instead, anyone who had three or four Jewish grandparents were defined or belonged to a Jewish community. Even Jews who had converted to Christianity were defined as Jews. Clearly, the marriage of Heinrich and Lilli was considered illicit.

Kristin continued to pursue the investigation, but it took many more months until the pieces of the puzzle began to fit. She learned that an aunt who was Lutheran had applied to have the child sent to Britain as an orphan. Because Sophie was born to a Lutheran mother and two of her grandparents were Lutheran, the permit was granted. This was helped by the fact that the Miller family in Britain promised to raise the child as an Anglican Christian.

Thus, Kristin now realized where she had obtained some of her Jewish genetic characteristics. Was it possible that other members of Heinrich's family were also full-blooded Jews and had carried these genes into Sophie? If so, then Lilli's genetic contribution would only be a small one, the major contribution would be from Heinrich's familial line.

But Kristin was still an Anglican, notwithstanding this history. Her mother was Christian and an Anglican family saved her from the Jewish Holocaust. She would remain a Christian for she fully approved of the Christian principles that protected her and were carried through the two generations following Sophie's adoption into the faith.

While Kristin was continuing her investigation, the Israeli military remained on high alert, waiting for any invasion or hint of another nuclear attack. But none occurred, a fact that only made the citizens of Israel and its government more paranoid and more insecure of the ensuing times.

The Prime Minister of Israel received no assurances of support from the United Nations. In fact, the UN continued to consider Israel a source of antagonism in the conflict despite the attack on its sovereignty. Communications between the president of the United States and the Prime Minister of Israel continued, but the U.S. did not move forward in this situation because it claimed that the party who had instigated the attack had not been identified. Therefore, the U.S. would not act until more evidence would be at hand. But the U.S. continued to warn Israel that it should not take any unilateral actions against any of its Middle East neighbors since doing so would put the U.S. in difficult circumstances, perhaps start a third world war.

During these ensuing months, David continued to survive the transplant and showed little evidence of any GVHD as long as he took his medications. The cortisone doses were decreased over time, and he only needed one medication to control the threat of GVHD. The hospital palliative care team that had given him psychosocial and spiritual support when he was near death came to see him less frequently. But Kristin would continue to visit him daily, and they would communicate through the isolation window that would, for these two dear friends, make the world a far more hospitable place.

Time ameliorates all wounds, and David was now getting ready to be discharged. But where would he go? Who would take care of him? Who would help him continue to heal his wounds? Who would heal Kristin's wounds?

CHAPTER X

I looked up and saw a bright smiling face. "Good morning, dear brother." It was Kristin.

M.S.PLATT   THE LAST SUPPER

"Well, good morning to you, dear sister. What brings you here so chipper this morning?"

"Have the doctors talked to you yet, David?"

"No. They are still making rounds down the hall. What's up?"

"Well. I'm not supposed to say anything, but one of the doctors wanted to know where you might be discharged. And I hope that you don't mind that I volunteered that you stay with me. I have plenty of room and Neville Boy is no problem. He is a dear. Never angry, never fussy. It is such a pleasure raising him. Well, David. Now that I let the cat out of the bag, what do you say?"

"What can I say? I do know that you are a dear and most generous friend. You know that I have hardly any family left in Israel. I don't want to go back to the States. I feel like I belong here in Israel. Thank God my insurance and pension funds in the States took over when this accident happened, so now I have enough money coming in. But I really don't have anywhere to go. Do you really want to take me?"

" David, David. You are like family to me now. I surely don't have any family in Israel. Rueben and Rivka have been dear, but they have their own personal needs. So, David, I guess *we* are family. Brother and sister now, caring for each other, and little Neville to boot! David, are you game? If they discharge you, I'll make all the arrangements."

"Kristin, I'm getting tired of this place. I *am* game. I need to find a new place and get well. And you are the person who could do it. I've missed you everyday when you leave from our visits. It will be nice to be home with you and Little Neville."

"Then it's a deal, David. I hear them close by making their rounds. I'll drop by later and find out what plans they have."

The hospital staff plan was to discharge me in a week. Kristin and the staff worked out the details. The medications were structured so that the doses could be reduced in time. And I would be seen at home for a twice-weekly blood test to measure the state of the transplant and any evidence of GVHD.

A week passes by quickly when you are having fun, and I was having fun anticipating my discharge. Kristin gathered new clothes for me. The staff put me in a wheel chair and I was off. Off to a new world. Off to new experiences. Off to a better life. The trip to Kristin's apartment was easy. She pushed me into the apartment in a wheel chair, and I rested the whole afternoon. When I awoke, she was watching me. Neville Boy, as she called him, was now six months old, and he was keeping busy in his playpen.

"Well, David. This is the diet they have planned for you. A nutritionist will contact us twice a week at first. Now let me tell you about our blood tests. You may not realize this, but we are *really* brother and sister now! I hope they told you that you have taken on some of my stem cells from Neville Boy's placenta and the other donor's placenta. Interestingly, the other donor's cells are rapidly decreasing. This happens in some double cord blood stem cell transfusions. But you can't get rid of *my* blood cells, dear brother! I am part of you now. You are now a chimera. David, do you know what a chimera is? Let me tell you. It is from Greek mythology and represents a composite of a lion, a goat, and a serpent. You, silly boy, are not any of these, but you are a composite of my son's stem cells, a few of the other donor's stem cells and your own cells. The numbers of each contributing cells are being tested regularly at

Rabin and matched to your clinical status. So now, dear love, you have some cells with Neville Boy's genes. But his genes were obtained from Neville, my husband, and me. As I told you in the hospital, I have a goodly number of Jewish traits in my genes, from of my grandmother Sophie and from her father. So tell me, my dear David. Doesn't that make you happy? We are all related! See I did all this research to let you know all this. We are related in many ways, dear soul. I wish that I had a chance to meet my grandmother, but she passed away several years ago. I would have so much wanted to discuss our family history with her. Perhaps she would not have known about those things. After all, she was but six years old when she was brought to Britain. Yet there is so much I want to learn."

"Kristin," I said hesitantly. "I did a lot of research while I was in the hospital. I had use of a computer, and I wondered why my family never wanted to discuss Treblinka with Grandfather Ari.
"Kristen… Kristin…. I now know. He was a prisoner at Treblinka, and he lost most of his family there. Although some deny the existence of the Holocaust, I am clearly aware of the Holocaust. I am a historian, and I know. A

whole generation of European Jews was annihilated in World War II, and Grandfather Ari was one of the survivors of that generation. I don't feel comfortable discussing that tragedy with you today, but I must.... I must share it with you.

"The Holocaust in Europe was no different than the Holocaust in Tel Aviv several months ago. Some one... some people plan to destroy the Jews. In World War II, we knew who the enemy was and did little to respond to the danger until it was too late. Now we don't even know who the enemy is. Can we respond this time to this present danger? I now know why no one discussed this with Grandfather Ari. But you and I need to discuss it. Some in your family were saved from the horrors of these murders. I need to disgorge the violence of those times. I need to try to deal with the violence of our present time. So this is what I learned:

"Treblinka was a death camp operated by Nazi officials in World War II from July 23, 1942 to October 19, 1943. It was 62 miles northeast of Warsaw and conveniently placed between the Warsaw Ghetto and the Bialystok Ghetto. During that interval, 870,000 people were killed, of which 800,000 were Jews. The intent of the Nazis was to destroy the Jews of the Warsaw Ghetto and the Jews in Poland. Treblinka consisted of two sections. Treblinka I was a forced labor camp where prisoners were forced to work in gravel pits and irrigation ditches. Over 20,000 people were killed from exhaustion, execution or mistreatment.

"Treblinka II was the more horrible of the two. It was a planned death factory. All or most of the prisoners were killed outright—usually within a day or two after arriving. The few survivors of Treblinka II were from labor units forced to bury victim's bodies in mass graves—and later—to cremate the corpses. These survivors were called the Sonderkommandos, and since Grandfather Ari survived that camp, he must have been one of them. He must had been a strong youth of 17 years of age and put to work, or else, he would have been killed with the rest of the people.

"Treblinka II was composed of three parts. The lower camp or Camp 2 was the receiving area where a railroad extended from the station into the camp. A portion of this camp housed the commanders' quarters and barracks for the 800 prisoners who operated the camp. Two barracks were near the railroad tracks and were

M.S.PLATT THE LAST SUPPER

used to store the belongings of the newly arrived prisoners. To these newly arriving Jews, it looked like a railroad station, even with a wooden clock at the gate. Two other buildings were used to undress the new arrivals. Women's clothes were removed and their hair was shorn. A cashier's office collected money and jewelry. A small barrack was situated nearby. It was painted white and even had a Red Cross on its wall. Sick, wounded, or dead prisoners were moved to this area. Behind the building, there was a ditch, and these prisoners would be moved to that area and shot in the head. Then their bodies would fall into the ditch.

"A third section--Camp 3 or upper camp-- was the real death camp. It was on a small hill. The prisoners who arrived on the trains would be led up the hill, stripped of their clothes and valuables, and then gassed in gas chambers. Behind each gas chamber was a large pit where bodies were placed on wooden rails and then cremated.

'The official guards of the camp were German or Austrian with a few additional Russians or Ukrainians. There were 700 to 800 Jewish prisoners, the specialized Sonderkommandos, who were divided into three groups. The Blue Squads unloaded the trains, carried the luggage, and cleaned the railroad wagon cars. The Red Squads undressed the prisoners and took the clothes to storage areas. The Geldjuden or 'money Jews' handled the money, gold, stocks and jewelry. A dentist would pull the gold from the teeth of dead bodies. The Totenjuden or 'Jews of death' would carry the dead from the gas chambers to a furnace. Over 90% of the prisoners sent to Treblinka died within the first two hours of arrival. Many of the Sonderkommandos committed suicide with their belts rather than continuing their hideous work. And it was said that the stench of the camp extended for over six miles into an adjacent village.

"By June 1943, the Sonderkommandos decided to rebel, but a mishap occurred in their plans and the rebellion was delayed until August 2. Fortunately, a group of German and Ukrainian guards drove off that morning to go swimming so there was fewer staff to resist the rebellion. The rebel Sonderkommandos unlocked a door to the weapons arsenal near the train tracks and stole rifles, grenades, and pistols. In thirty minutes, the insurgency began. Buildings were set on fire. A tank of petrol was exploded, and the main gate was attacked. Many of the Sonderkommandos climbed the camp fence but were machine-gunned by the Germans. About 200 escaped. Half of these were later captured and killed. The remaining 100 who did escape fled into the nearby woods and later joined the Polish Resistance Army. After the war, some of these moved to Israel. Grandfather Ari must have been one of them. Treblinka was kept in operation by the Nazis for a few more months, but then was closed forever.

"Kristin. I think about this, and I think about what is going on now in Israel and Palestine. The Jews need a homeland free of adversity. It may be true that Arabs in Israel, Gaza, or the West Bank may complain of improper treatment, but none of them…none of them… ever experienced the trauma of Treblinka or any of the German exterminating camps of World War II. The problem of partition of these lands in Israel and Palestine is resolvable if the parties agree or are forced to agree to partition. But one thing I do know. The Jews will not passively allow themselves to be exterminated again as in World War II or as in the deluge in Tel Aviv."

I lowered my head and became silent.

Suddenly the phone began to ring incessantly. Kristin picked it up.

"Hello. Hello. Dr. Hudson here."

"Is this Dr. Hudson?"

"Yes. Yes. What is it?"

"This is the hospital calling. Rabin Medical Center. You need to come to the Center immediately. There has been an explosion at two of the nuclear processing centers in Iran. The Israeli government and military are on full alert. You must come to the hospital and be prepared for any emergent consequences. Please leave your home. Come to your station at the Center immediately. Have your family go to the shelters."

Kristin looked at me. She had a quizzical look on her face and quickly explained the situation to me.

"I love you, Kristin."

"I love you too, David. Take care of Neville Boy if I don't come back."

Then she hugged Neville Boy and me, and disappeared into the darkness of the night.

CHAPTER XI

 I gently picked up baby Neville. "Come on little fellow. We'd better get ourselves to the shelter. It's cold out there, but I will hold you close to me and protect you from the night wind. We must be careful, for I must not fall. I may be weak, but I cannot fall. You and I, Neville Boy, must be strong. For your mom… For us… I love you so. I love you both so."

 I wrapped Neville Boy in two blankets and slowly managed the stairwell to the street. Fortunately the shelter was in the adjacent apartment basement, and we entered through a dimly lit entranceway. Neville Boy somehow remained silent and asleep. How peaceful and pleasant he was! And I was grateful. I found a small bench and sat down with Neville on my lap. The shelter was beginning to fill up, and it soon became crowded.

 "What a lovely baby you have there," a middle aged woman sitting next to me said. "Where is your wife?"

 "Wife…? Oh, there is no…" I hesitated for a moment. I loved Kristin so much now. And we *were* like family together. Why not? I realized now that Kristin should be my wife. I wanted that. I wanted that more than anything in life.

M.S.PLATT   THE LAST SUPPER

"Oh, she works at the Rabin Hospital and had to report for duty." I had lied, but I really wanted Kristin to be my wife."

"I'm sure you must be proud of her," she responded. "Everyone must help at these times. My own son is in the army."

More people entered the shelter, and it began to get steamy. I thought of the Nazi railroad cars carrying the Jews to Treblinka and the hot, cramped people in them. I thought of the residents of London huddled in their underground shelters in World War II, ever oblivious to the bombing and fires above them. But they survived because they had purpose and strength, and I resolved to have a similar purpose and strength. For this little child in my arms. For Kristin.

The Warden soon began passing out small cartons of orange juice. Someone even brought a bottle of warm milk for Neville Boy. He eagerly accepted the milk, and I rejoiced. I felt like I was really feeding my own child.

In the quiet of the shelter, in the quiet of the night, we began to fall asleep, even in upright positions. I tried to be attentive so that I would not drop my little boy, and would lean against the damp cool wall to keep steady. I tried not to hold him too tightly, for I remembered that holding a baby too tightly could be dangerous. One could compromise a baby's respiration. So I would change my position periodically and relax my hold on him. He would awaken and stare at me with his big beautiful blue-green eyes…Kristin's eyes. How I loved looking into those eyes!

I thought of the love lives of Kristin and Neville in London. How Neville had changed! How he must have loved this woman. And now I realized that I held in my arms a product of that love. And I was happy for this little boy.

How complicated this world had now become. "Little Neville, I love you so. I loved your father. How I loved your father, and he loved me. We would huddle together in the cold rooms at college. How we survived then, I do not know. And here I am now hugging you. You, who is part me; and I, who am part of you. Part your father. Part your mother. Whom do I love now? Are we not all brothers in this world? Whom do I love? Do I love myself? Isn't it time for me to start loving myself?"

I bent my head down and kissed Little Neville's forehead. He awoke and stared at me. To him I was a stranger, but a stranger who would assure him of safety in this hostile world.

"Little man, I miss your mother. I *love* your mother. I hope she returns, for I need her. She needs me, and you, my beloved child, need us both. I shall always be here for you, to protect you. To see you grow in the image of your father, my beloved. I loved your father, and now I love you. We are all together again. Where are you, dear Neville? Where do you travel in Paradise?"

After a full night, the alarm was sounded that all was clear, and we were advised that we could return to our homes. I gathered up Neville Boy and carefully moved up the stairwell. As I got to the street level, the bright morning sun startled and awakened me. Autos were beginning to move about the streets, and I worked my way to the apartment and opened the door. Kristin had not yet returned so I lay Neville Boy in his crib and fell soundly asleep on the floor.

I don't know how long I slept, but later that afternoon, I heard the door lock open. I looked up anxiously, frightened that an intruder had entered. But that was illogical. Only Kristin and I had keys to the door. How happy I was to see her. She looked tired, but I jumped up to touch her, to greet her, to welcome her home. I had missed her so.

"Happy to see you, Kristin. I have fed Neville Boy and changed his diaper."

"How did you do that? Do you know how to change a diaper, David? You are so sweet."

" I've learned by watching you, dear girl. I'm getting a little housebroken, I guess. Busy last night at the hospital?"

"No. We stayed at our stations but had nothing to do. No casualties. They dismissed us this morning. How was the shelter?"

"Crowded and damp, but we survived. Little Neville slept through most of it. The Warden even gave me some milk to feed him. Hear anything about what is going on?"

"Only rumors. Apparently the bombs that went off in Iran created a large radioactive cloud. The Iranians have closed their borders and are delaying the UN Atomic Energy Inspection teams. They claim that according to the treaty they have a 24-day delay before the inspectors can come to inspect. I don't know if the UN will be so lenient. Something fishy is going on in Iran. As long as they aren't bombing us, I guess we should be grateful. At least World War III has not begun."

The UN teams pressed the issue of inspection and entered Iran. This was helped by the fact that Russia was getting agitated because the nuclear dust had passed over the Caucasian Mountains and had moved northward over Moscow.

The Shin Bet Internal Security Service and Mossad Intelligence Agency confirmed to the Israeli Ministers of Defense and Interior that two low yield atomic weapons had exploded at the surface of two nuclear research entities in Iran, south of Tehran—at the Natanz and Fordo uranium enrichment facilities. Interestingly, the Bushehr nuclear reactor near the Persian Gulf was not struck. Similar to the Hiroshima bomb in 1945, a sixty thousand feet tall nuclear mushroom cloud developed at the two sites and a two-mile diameter of destruction had enveloped all the surface buildings, personnel and developments. The event occurred at about 2 A.M., Tehran time. As in Hiroshima, there was considerable loss of life and property, and the mushroom cloud was now dissipating nuclear dust and debris into the cosmopolitan areas of Tehran. The downward fallout was not yet defined but appeared to be positioned with the prevalent winds toward the Caspian Sea, the Caucasus Mountains and northward toward Russia, taking a similar path—north, northwest—as had the radioactive fallout after the Chernobyl explosion in 1986. There was also concern that the downwind fallout might shift eastward. If the downward fallout did shift eastward, it would be directed thousands of miles across Afghanistan, Pakistan and India, potentially killing hundreds of thousands of people two weeks after the explosion and exposing another 35 million to cancer-causing radiation.

   Radioactive fallout is the particulate matter or dust that is produced by a nuclear explosion and carried high up into the air by the mushroom cloud. It drifts on the wind and most of it settles back to earth downward from the explosion. The heaviest, most dangerous and most noticeable fallout falls closer to ground zero usually arriving minutes after the explosion. The smaller and lighter dust-like particles drift much farther, often for hundreds of miles and for many weeks. It coats everything on the ground and appears as a fine, grit-like dust. However, any rain that would be above the Caspian Sea could concentrate the fallout into localized 'hot-spots' of more intense radiation and carry the radioactive particles for greater distances. Radioactive dust can contain dangerous elements of alpha, beta, and penetrating gamma radiation. The latter can penetrate through walls, roofs and protective clothing. Even though the fallout dissipates in the air and undergoes natural decay over time, it is still highly dangerous.

At first, the Iranian government did not issue any reports. It did seal all of its borders, closed all communication channels, rounded up all foreigners and diplomats and placed them under detention and preliminary arrest.

The issue was whether a low level atomic explosion at the Iranian research facility could itself create a substantial explosion. Was the amount of highly enriched uranium at these two research facilities sufficient to do this? That notion appeared to be unlikely since at least 55 pounds of enriched uranium would be needed to create such a weapon, although some authorities maintained that as little as 6 pounds would do it.

M.S.PLATT   THE LAST SUPPER

Could a missile strike cause nuclear material in the facilities to explode? It was argued that if a large missile struck the arsenal, no chain reaction would ensue. A chain reaction would be needed because a nuclear detonation requires a highly choreographed series of explosions within a few microseconds in order to simultaneously compress uranium or plutonium within all sides of a missile. Absent such an event, the facility nuclear materials would not detonate.

No one adequately explained why the Bushehr nuclear reactor was not hit. Perhaps this was because Russia was now involved with Bushehr. Certainly, Iran was not eager to discuss the work done at Bushehr. The Bushehr entity was important. It had been built and supplied with the help of the Russian government who contributed the uranium isotope nuclear fuel. It was well known that uranium reactors could be used to produce plutonium.

The Iranian nuclear deal with the United States and the world powers stipulated that Iran's uranium stockpile would be reduced by 98% for 15 years. The level of uranium enrichment would remain at 3.67%.

M.S.PLATT   THE LAST SUPPER

The uranium enrichment facility at Natanz would be limited and the facility at Fordo curtailed for 15 years.

Plutonium is an atomic byproduct of uranium, and the Bushehr facility could produce it. Sub-atomic neutrons produced in the uranium reactor fuel rods split atoms of uranium in two and release energy, more neutrons and multiplying chain reactions. The remaining uranium atoms in the fuel rods absorb the additional neutrons and turn into plutonium. In fact, Iran had experimented with plutonium bombs previously but had agreed in the recent treaty to forego plutonium production. Although a plutonium explosion would yield less energy than a uranium type bomb, the dispersion of highly radioactive fallout from plutonium would be greater. These would make less "noise" but be highly more dangerous especially if exploded in a place like New York harbor. Was Iran sending uranium or plutonium to Natanz or Fordo?

These questions needed to be answered quickly. Many of the Western countries, including the United States, had surveillance capabilities. Thus, the United States who had a nuclear bomb limitation treaty with Iran immediately contacted the government of Iran and demanded release of the U.S. diplomatic officers. The United States also forwarded a number of inquiries to the International Atomic Energy Agency who was supposed to monitor the Iranian "peaceful" use of nuclear energy. Obviously, this agency as well as the previous U.S. federal agencies and officers that had negotiated the Iran nuclear agreement were embarrassed by the situation in Iran, but the present U.S. administration was adamant. Not only did the U.S. press the Iranian government and the United Nations, it was wary of Israel. Immediate channels were opened up between the president of the U.S. and the prime minister of Israel. When abruptly and impolitely confronted by the U.S. president, the Israeli prime minister strongly denied that its government had any involvement with the nuclear attack on Iranian soil. It pleaded innocence, claiming that it had promised the U.S. government that it would withhold any attacks and pointed out, with logic and clear reason, that the U.S. military was actively involved in Israeli defense and would have easily known in advance if the Israeli military or secret service agency had any plans for such an attack. The Israelis invited the U.S. military advisors to join the Israeli defense teams and covert secret service elements to review the activities of the Israeli forces so as to prove that Israel had "clean hands" in this matter. Criticism by other western powers, even Russia, was also an issue. These parties claimed that the U.S. was protecting Israel and that both the U.S. and Israel must "own up" to this terrible act and pay retribution to Iran as well as the rest of the world. The Arab nations quickly joined in with the chorus of accusations, but the U.S. pressed on since no one, as noted in the Tel Aviv attack, had claimed responsibility for the act.

The U.S., in concert with the UN, began an aggressive investigation into the circumstances. What did these parties learn? Tracking information from U.S. submarines in the Persian Gulf indicated that two missiles were launched at approximately 2 A.M. on the night of the attack. The perpetrators of the launches quickly fled the scene. There were no aircraft in the area so the assumption was that a small submarine made the launches. It did not use sophisticated equipment and remained undetected when it entered the Persian Gulf. The path, as well as the home base, of the alleged submarine could not be detected and remained unknown. This surreptitious act was similar to the one performed in the Mediterranean Sea just west of Tel Aviv on Passover Eve. Again, who could be the suspects?

1. Turkey and Cyprus were low on the list. They had nothing to gain.
2. Egypt and Libya or terrorist groups in their countries could have performed the act, but did not appear sophisticated enough in the weaponry to perform the strikes.
3. Iran certainly would not attack its own soil.
4. Israel, as usual, was high on the list, notwithstanding the evidence that it did not perform the strikes.
5. The Islamic State of Iraq and Syria (ISIS), a belligerent terrorist group that had been fighting in Syria and parts of Iraq, was considered. It did have a sophisticated group of officers from the previous Baathist Saddam Hussein administration, but it was unclear if it had the

financial resources. It was well known that Iran and ISIS were at war with each other. It was also known that Saudi Arabia was at odds with Iran, in part, because of the competition for oil sales and revenue in the Middle East. Observers noted that the Saudi were Sunni and the Iranians were Shi'ite and bitter opponents in their practice of Islam. Did the Saudis support the venture?
6. Did North Korea sell the atomic weapons to any of the adversaries?
7. Although Pakistan had mixed populations of Sunni and Shi'ite, it had nuclear capabilities, and its naval forces included some submarines that were capable of nuclear warhead trajectory.
8. Russia was an ally of Iran and would not be suspect.

M.S.PLATT   THE LAST SUPPER

Absent any group that claimed the attack, the UN, the U.S. and the European nations were no better off than when they investigated the Tel Aviv attack.

Tensions in the world increased. The Arab nations in the Middle East claimed that the U.S. and Western Europe were technically at war with them and promised recriminations. The U.S. and western European nations prepared for attacks by various terrorist organizations that had acted previously in Paris, Belgium, Britain and Spain. The U.S. Congress began to rebuild its military power and took on increasing debt in the process.

U. S. and worldwide Evangelists watched in awe. Had not the signs of the end of the world, as prophesized by Peter in 2 Peter 3, become evident? The Evangelists listed the events that would precede the world's demise and discussed them with mixed anxiety:

    1. The world had witnessed a rapid increase of knowledge as evidenced by the massive use of cell phones and electronic tablets and the growth of genetics and the science of DNA.

2. There had now been an exponential increase in personal and national debt.
3. There was an increase in violence, murders, and sexual immorality.
4. The world had experienced marked increases in natural disasters such as floods, earthquakes, tornados, and famine.
5. There was widespread evidence of a departure by many people from the doctrines of the Christian Faith and an increase in occult practices and spiritualism. Were not immoral and fantasy cinema and TV clearly abundant?
6. War was now a constant threat. Armageddon and atomic devastation were soon to come.

These events were similar to the prophesy of Peter: "Soon the heavens will disappear and the earth and everything will be destroyed by fire. All that God had created will be destroyed. There will be an explosion that will consume and obliterate all matter, as we know it. ONLY THEN WILL GOD CREATE A NEW HEAVEN AND EARTH. AND ONLY THEN WILL THE HOLY SAVIOR, THE MESSIAH, BE RAISED FROM THE DEAD AND SAVE US.

The Evangelists waited anxiously, joyfully and expectantly.

Chapter XII

In this milieu Kristin, Neville Baby, and I waited in a crucible of fire between the dominions of the Middle East and the dominions of the West.

"David," Kristin asked. "Do you think there can be any resolution to this conflict? Is the world facing a world war and nuclear annihilation?"

"Kristin I don't know. But I do know that both the Middle East and the Western nations will need to accommodate. They can accommodate, but the question is whether they wish to accommodate before they destroy us all. I am a historian, and I know how mankind has mistreated this planet. I know how humanity treats the God that it allegedly serves. And it all began here in this fertile crescent of civilization, this

M.S.PLATT   THE LAST SUPPER

Garden of Eden, where the notion of an omnipotent God originated.

"But mankind has learned one thing in its existence on this earth: How to destroy itself, how to destroy the vestiges of great civilizations.

"It is a world that does not love God, nor understand Him, or even listen to Him.

"It is a world where people are subjugated and enslaved by masters.

"It is a world where God is used as a symbol.

"And the masters who use God, attain political, economic, mosque, and church power to overwhelm the Children of God by elaborate theocracies,

"And then concentrate their power –ALL IN THE NAME OF GOD.

"And, Kristin, neither the West or the East is innocent of these travesties. Let me share some of my study of history with you:

"*Homo sapiens,* our human species, has been on this planet for about 200,000 years, but began to exhibit evidence of modernity about 50,000 years ago. Although the species was first sustained by hunting and gathering, it began to form human settlements, domesticate plants and animals, and use metal tools. Then its societies established various forms of government, religion, and culture. These early cradles of civilization began in Mesopotamia, within the fertile crescent of the Middle East, and elsewhere in China-India. But humankind has not known any peace. The nations of the Fertile Crescent have always been at war. Neville, Abram, my cousin, and I discussed these issues on the night that the tsunami struck. The religious priests of these nations joined with their kings and dominated their indigenous populations as well as the people they conquered. They formed theocracies where religious doctrine and priest rule were the law of the land. This situation hasn't changed much in the history of mankind. Let me share some of these theocratic nations' histories with you:

ISLAM

"Throughout history, theocracies have ruled the nation states of the Middle East. These Islamic nations do not practice freedom of religion, a basic right of humanity.

M.S.PLATT   THE LAST SUPPER

"Two factors highlight the conflict between Islamic East and Christian West. The first is the basic firmness of the Qur'an and the interpretations of the Qur'an in the Hadith. The Qur'an is the word of Allah, the God of the Muslims, as conveyed to Muhammad, their Prophet. And it is in the Qur'an that Muhammad advises His followers—often, and repetitively: A true Arab believer of Allah must act with courage and honor to protect his religion, his home and his land—or else, the purgatory fires of Satan will claim him. Every sura, every aya (every section, every verse) is a constant reminder of this theme. These religious documents spell out the daily practices that are expected of all Muslims. There is little, if any, flexibility in these dictates. Muslims consider Western cultures and legal rules to be inferior, degenerate, and evil. The second factor was the loss by the Muslim Ottoman Empire of control of Mesopotamia and Palestine to the Western powers following World War I. An Arab never forgets defeat and always waits patiently...patiently for a time to correct it. Mesopotamia may now be in the hands of Muslims, but the loss of this land to the Western Powers in 1918 to 1922 would never be forgotten. In fact, the control of

M.S.PLATT   THE LAST SUPPER

Palestine by the British and of Mesopotamia by the French was never acceptable to the Arabs. Revolts by the Arabs finally allowed Islam to regain control of Mesopotamia. Islam ultimately claimed revenge on the West when vast quantities of oil were found in these lands. The profits from oil were initially channeled into Sheikhdoms and were used for personal, political and economic intrigues. Pan-Arabism grew following World War II as a counter-reaction to these intrigues, but this movement was overtaken by the ambitions of various oppressive dictators. The response to these dictators and the formation of the state of Israel was replaced with Islamic hostility to the West and with terrorism in Israel. Pro-Arab apologists such as Edward Said of Columbia University preached to the West that English and French colonialism was evil; and the liberal wings of America and the West accepted this sermon without reflection or serious analysis. Another writer, Bernard Lewis, favored the Ataturk model in Turkey after World War I. Lewis advocated democracy in the Middle East. Sadly to say, the Islamic culture of tribe, clan and adversity never accepted democracy as a model. Rarely has it been successful.

M.S.PLATT   THE LAST SUPPER

"The overarching problem with Islam is one of history. Islam has controlled the Middle East since 620 CE when Muhammad first communicated with Allah, taught the religion to the nomadic people of the Arabian Peninsula, and, with His followers, guided these people to conquer all the lands from Spain to India. Islam has dominated this vast area under various regimes: Sunni, Shia, Ottoman Empire. Even the Mongol invaders of the 13th Century converted to Islam. Thus, Islam and the West have an irresolvable confrontation. Islam is the supreme culture of the Middle East.

"Consider the two dominant nations of the Middle East: Saudi Arabia and Iran. Saudi Arabia is an Islamic theocracy. Islam is the state religion of Saudi Arabia, and its laws require that all its citizens to be Muslim. The government does not legally protect the freedom of religion. In fact, it has a poor human rights record. Religious minorities do not have the right to practice their religion. Non-Muslim propagation is banned, and the conversion from Islam to another religion is considered an apostasy and is punishable by death. The distribution of non-Muslim religious material such as the Christian Bible is illegal. Wahhabism is the version of Islam in Saudi Arabia. This religion is a branch of Sunni Islam, but it is very ultraconservative. The Saudi Kingdom proclaimed Wahhabism a state-sponsored official form of Sunni Islam in 1932, and it serves as its religion in the 21st Century. Many Sunni or Shia do not accept the Wahhabi movement. With the help of funding from petroleum exports, Wahhabism underwent explosive growth beginning in the 1970's and has worldwide influence. Wahhabism has been accused of being a source of global terrorism and inspires adherents of ISIS. The success of the petroleum industries in the Middle East has prompted the West to become dependent on these products. Entrepreneurs in the West have preferred to satisfy their greed to gain wealth while their nations suffer under this dependency. The use of fossil fuels in the West is addictive just as opium/heroin is addictive to an adolescent juvenile. There will be little resistance in the West to counteract this addiction. Prominent business entrepreneurs will benefit from the sale of fossil fuels just like any other drug dealer sells his product anywhere in the world.

M.S.PLATT   THE LAST SUPPER

"Iran has adopted the Shi'ite form of Islam and stands in direct opposition to Sunni cultures. As in Saudi Arabia, minorities are denied certain religious rights. Shia is the official state religion, and all its laws and regulations must be based on Islamic criteria and official interpretations of Sharia, the legal code of many Islamic states. Although Zoroastrians, Jews and Christians may worship in Iran, proselytizing is prohibited, and their worship is constrained by public opinion. Several members of the Bahia community have been executed. Christians Protestants practice in secret. The government discriminates against all religious minority groups in employment, education, and housing. The Iranians have supported the Shia communities in southern Iraq and have been accused of terrorist activities in many areas of the Middle East. It supports terror in Israel and propagates that Israel be destroyed.

"The Iranian interest in developing 'peaceful' nuclear energy has been an issue, and a recent international treaty has given Iranian scientists the ability to move forward in this area. However, there remains concern as to the motives of the Iranians. The presence of nuclear weaponry in any Islamic nation's military arsenal foretells a serious dilemma. Any terrorist organization that has use of these weapons will become an opponent and potential victor against the Western cultures of Europe and America.

"Unfortunately, modern Islamists do not pay attention to Sura 2:256 of the Qur'an:

> 'Let here be no compulsion in religion: true guidance has become distinct from error, so whoever rejects false gods and believes in God has grasped the firmest hand-hold, one that will never break.'

"And Sura 42:15:

> 'I believe in whatever Scripture God has sent down. I am commanded to bring justice between you. God is our Lord and your Lord to us our deeds and to you your deeds, so let there be no argument between us and you.'

" Thus, there is a path for accommodation between the faiths. In fact, the early Muslims conquered many nations by accommodating to other faiths and cultures.

It was later in Islamic history that Muslims began to be hostile to them."

JUDAISM

"Yahweh, the God of the Jews, through Moses their Prophet, gave them the Torah and all the 613 Commandments therein. The signal contribution of Judaism was the Decalogue or Ten Commandments. These serve as a foundation for most modern civilizations and religions. Most of the other commandments in the Torah can become complex and demanding save for the recognition of a single God and observing the Sabbath and certain festivals. Judaism is an ancient monotheistic religion, and its early history was that of a theocratic society that was intolerant of other religions. References in the Old Testament depict brutal treatment of the Canaanites, Midianites, and other cultures.

"The priests in early Israel performed animal sacrifices in their Temple in Jerusalem and maintained strict religious, ritualistic authority over its people. In time, the Temple was destroyed after several tumultuous wars. The Romans finally destroyed the

M.S.PLATT THE LAST SUPPER

Second Temple in 70 CE. Rabbinic Judaism emerged as the official religion thereafter and incorporated the Midrash and Talmud as later supplemental religious traditions. The sacrificial practices were terminated and replaced by prayer. Most orthodox Jews attempt to follow these traditions, but modern Jews do not adhere to all 613 Commandments. Non-Jews who wish to convert to Judaism are dissuaded, for Judaism is a difficult religion; converts may find the challenge impossible. Non-Orthodox Jews such as the Conservative, Reformed, or Reconstructionist branches of Judaism do not adhere to all the 613 Commandments. Ultra-Orthodox Jews in Israel do not approve of these divergent practices, for they follow the Commandments with a passion. These serve as a fence to protect them from the outside world. Do these Jews realize that this protective fence might become their ghetto walls similar to those of their central European communities?

"Judaism has survived multiple attempts at its annihilation, but remains an important and active role in the modern world, perhaps, in part, because of its contributions to the world's civilizations and as an example of a moral society. However, as a result of the

M.S.PLATT   THE LAST SUPPER

Holocaust in Europe during World War II, approximately 50% of the Jews in the world live in Israel. For these Jews, Israel has become the homeland for many of the Diaspora Jews. The Israeli constitution maintains freedom of religious practice for all of its citizens, but ultra-Orthodoxy has become an issue within the state. If ultra-Orthodoxy becomes dominant in modern Israel, the nation that espouses freedom of religion will no longer have this freedom, and it too could become a theocracy. Presently, however, Israel remains the most democratic nation in the Middle East."

CHRISTIANITY

"Christianity began with the teachings of Jesus Christ, Himself a Jew, as were His Disciples. Christians believe that Jesus is the Son of God and the savior of humanity whose coming as the Messiah (the Christ) was prophesized in the Old Testament. They also believe that Jesus suffered, died and rose from the dead, and they believe in the Trinity doctrine. This holds that God is three consubstantial persons: God, the Father; Jesus Christ, the Son; and the Holy Spirit. Christians believe that Jesus reigns with God, the Father, and that He will return to judge the living and the dead and grant eternal life to His followers.

"Early Christianity was practiced by Jews and Gentiles who adopted the faith. In time, the Gentiles became the only believers, but there were multiple sects. Initially, Christianity was an illicit faith, but spread rapidly after Constantine recognized it in 313 CE. It became the solely authorized religion in Rome in 380 CE. Constantine used the religion to gain theological, political, and economic power of the Roman Empire. Constantine and his followers abolished alleged heretic sects and organized the religion by adopting the Nicene Creed in 325 CE. The Church became more powerful following the adoption of the Niceno-Constantinopolitan Creed in 381CE.   Christianity became the dominant religion, and other faiths were ostracized or oppressed. The religion spread throughout Asia Minor and Europe, and Constantinople became the capital city of the Byzantine (Roman) Empire. Differences in theology, religious practice, and politics caused a schism of the Eastern and Western Christian Churches in 1054 CE, but each remained theocratic. The ruling classes and the Church supported the feudal societies of the Middle Ages. The Magna Carta actually protected the interests of the Barons and Church, not the serfs. The serfs only gained a few rights after the Black Plague had decimated their population, and the land gentry needed laborers to perform the menial duties of life in that day.

"Christianity has always been described as a peaceful religion, but its history points to another conclusion. Consider the Crusades of the 11th to 15th Centuries. Pope Urban initiated the first Crusade in 1095 CE in order to resist the advances of the Muslims in the Holy Land and to protect Constantinople. Peasants and nobles alike volunteered in order to satisfy feudal obligations and seek propitiation for their sins. However, during the course of the various Crusades, the Jews of the Rhineland were massacred, Constantinople was sacked and its inhabitants annihilated, and various Eastern Christian communities were destroyed and their lands confiscated. Some Crusades were used to destroy alleged heretic groups within the Church in Cather France, the Hussites in Bohemia, and the Iberian peninsula. They also set the foundation for the Inquisitions later on. The Crusades did open the

M.S.PLATT   THE LAST SUPPER

Mediterranean for trade and expanded the exchange of knowledge in literature, hygiene and philosophy between the West and East. However, domination of the Holy Land by the West was only transient. In time, the Middle East was recaptured by the Muslims and remained in their hands until the end of World War I.

"Following the Schism of 1054 CE, the Eastern and Western Latin Churches excommunicated each other and have remained separate despite an attempt to reunite in the 20th Century. Compared to the western Latin Church, the Eastern Orthodox Church has no papacy or similar authority and geographically resides in Greece, Eastern Europe, Russia and a few communities in the Middle East.

"A further breach of the Christian Church occurred during the Reformation of the 16th Century wherein Protestantism came into existence. Following the Reformation, nation states followed the religion of the ruler, but, in the main, these were Roman Catholic in the southern tier of Europe and Protestant in the north.

"Following the Age of Enlightenment, the degree and nature of a government backing a denomination as a state religion varied. It could range from mere endorsement of a denomination with freedom for other faiths to practice, or prohibiting any competing religious body from operating, or persecuting the followers of other sects. Following he Age of Enlightenment, the notion of freedom of religious practice gained accession. A church's status as an organ of the state was repealed, and this gained popularity in the West."

"David. Sweet, David. What a wonderful exposition of history you have presented. Now, how about listening from a woman's point of view? I know that you look at Jesus differently than I do. You are Jewish. I am Christian. You men gave the world the Old Testament and the burden of the original sin. Poor Eve! Blamed for everything. And Adam got off, scot-free. What is wrong with knowledge? Is taking from the Tree of Knowledge that bad? It's what one does with that knowledge that makes a difference in life.

"For men, it has rendered that sorry history that you described: wars, economic and social injustice, dominance over human beings. For Jews and Muslims, knowledge gave them a fear of God. Knowledge was conveyed as sin. And sin is guilt and death. It gave humans the use of malevolent science. It gave men the power to use nuclear warfare.

" For some men, knowledge of God equated to being a God. Man tried to emulate God, to act like God, to compete with God. Man believed that he could keep people alive, even when their bodies failed and were close to death. Look at all the resuscitative measures now used in hospitals. Look at all the aggressive chemotherapy used when bodies are ravaged by cancer. But God does not play this game with Man. *In Creation, God created Nature as well as Man.* Human beings are at the mercy of nature and the changes of nature. And the path for nature is death. And death is the final arbiter of life. Man must accept that fate, for God will prevail.

"Jesus came to free the world from the burden of original sin. Jesus said:

 'Do not think that I have come to abolish the Law of Moses or the prophets. No. I have come to fulfill them.

 'Love the Lord your God with all your heart, with all your soul.... This is the First and Greatest Commandment, and a Second is like it. Love thy neighbor as thyself. All the Law and the prophets hang on these two Commandments.'

"So don't you see, dear, David? Knowledge of God is the key to finding God. The medieval philosophers taught that if we loved God, if we searched for God, we would find the peace and happiness that God bestows. It is finding the beauty of nature. For nature is the beauty of birth, of life, of death. It is the adversity and promise of living. It is the victory of pleasure over pain. Nature is the dualism of life's experiences. And Jesus gave us the path for the fulfillment of that life. The love of God and of His fellow human beings is the path of that fulfillment. That is what the early Christians sought and experienced: community and caring, sharing, the freedom to love one another, and to accept women as co-equal members of the community. That is what the early Christians practiced until the Roman dominated priests and emperors excommunicated any dissidents, and the church became a male oriented, organized hierarchy. Whereas women were accepted within the early church and spread the gospel, they were now relegated to a lessor status, and their efforts minimized. As such, this male controlled church has retained power for 1700 years. And so have war, greed and economic and political domination over simple human souls. Except for one thing that awakened the world and brought a hint that Jesus had again touched the minds and hearts of its inhabitants.

"It was a time in Western Europe during the 16th and 17th Centuries that thinkers like Frances Bacon, Rene Descartes, John Locke, David Hume and Adam Smith augmented a change in world history, and it was called the Age of Enlightenment.

THE AGE OF ENLIGHTENMENT

" The Age of Enlightenment included a range of ideas that centered on reason as a primary source of authority and came to promote the ideals of liberty, progress, tolerance, constitutional government and the separation of church and state. These prompted opposition to the principles of an absolute monarchy and the concept of the feudal divine right of kings. And these ideas spread to the American colonies. Benjamin Franklin, Thomas Jefferson, and many of the Founding Fathers adopted these ideals and incorporated them into the U.S. Declaration of Independence and Constitution.

"Does 'We hold these truths to be self evident, that all men are created equal, that they are endowed by their Creator with certain unalienable Rights, that among these are Life, Liberty and the pursuit of Happiness' sound familiar? Or the first amendment to the Constitution: 'Congress shall make no law respecting an establishment of religion, or the free exercise thereof….

"Freedom of religion was considered to be a fundamental right, and governments should permit the religious practices of other sects and not prosecute believers of other faiths. The separation of church and state was prompted by the principle of a social contract between citizens and their government.

"David. Your people in the United States have a problem. Although the constitution never mentioned slavery until the 13th amendment was passed, the economic practice of slavery prevailed for 76 years and was not completely addressed until 1965 with the Civil Rights Acts. Doesn't that sound like an anomaly with Jesus' teaching to love thy neighbor? You profess to have freedom of religion, yet your Christian churches preach that marriage with a same sex partner is prohibited. You rely on a state's right to control the moral activities of its citizens yet you try to limit a women's right to protect her body and her health. Don't misunderstand me. I do recognize that a woman should honor the life of her unborn child after it becomes viable. You even economically demean women by paying them less wages and dampen their educational opportunities. Are these signs of loving thy neighbor? Where is Jesus in the Christian Churches of America?"

"Kristin. My country is working on these deficiencies. Maybe the United States needs more time in accepting the true merits of the age of enlightenment. Maybe the true Christians in our society need to re-examine their faith.

" But, Kristin, the ideals of the enlightenment are a greater problem for Islam. Islam has not incorporated most of the ideals of the enlightenment. In fact, the enlightenment may be in direct conflict with the teachings of the Qur'an. An issue may arise whether Islamic culture can ever consider them. As I mentioned earlier, Bernard Lewis used the model of Ataturk who reorganized and secularized 20th Century Turkey in

M.S.PLATT   THE LAST SUPPER

1922. Lewis advocated this democratic formulation, but it failed to materialize in the Middle East. Some pro-Arab writers claim that the Arab countries need time to deal with these issues and note that the age of enlightenment took over 100 years to develop in Europe. These writers suggest that Islamic cultures be given a reasonable period of time to adjust to, experiment with, or reject the freedoms promoted by the enlightenment. Readers of the Qur'an can find avenues of flexibility in the words of the Prophet Mohammad. The Qur'an actually contains elements of brotherly love. The question then becomes whether members of the Islamic faith can find avenues of change within the confines of the Qur'an while giving full faith and observance to the Prophet. Muhammad even recognized the contributions of the 'People of the Book', the religions of the Jews and Christians. Clearly, a respectful dialogue with members of Islam and the West is necessary. Is that possible? At present, there does not appear to be any avenues open for communication. The economics of the petroleum industry, terrorism and the conflicts that exist between the dominions of the East and dominions of the West raise a deep sense of pessimism that dialogue will ever ensue unless the economic and political agendas of the East and West are re-examined."

CHAPTER XIII

"Hello. This is the United States Department of State calling the State Departments of England, France, Russia and China. The situation in the Middle East is getting out of hand. There is a risk of a World War III and a Nuclear Holocaust that will destroy the earth and all living matter. Since we are the five nations with a nuclear non-proliferation treaty and are highly susceptible to terrorist activity, we have a legitimate reason to meet and discuss this matter. The president of the United States wishes to meet the prime ministers of our five nations to explore viable options before a serious mishap occurs. We already have evidence that the explosions in Tel Aviv and Tehran were not well planned. We suggest a meeting in one week in Moscow so that the president and prime ministers of our countries and their staffs can set a path to avoid a worldwide catastrophe. Do you agree to meet? Respond accordingly.

M.S.PLATT   THE LAST SUPPER

ONE WEEK LATER. MEETING IN MOSCOW.

Prime Minister/Russia: Welcome to Moscow. My staff has reviewed some of your findings. We agree that the situation could become grave, and a response is quite necessary.

President/ United States: My nation appreciates the concerns that all of you have shown. We are willing to discuss the matter. What more do we know?

Prime Minister France: We have more tension in our country. As you know, terrorist attacks have occurred in some of our major cities. We have been able to subdue many of these, but the potential for more can occur. I have information that London and Edinburgh are due for attacks.

Prime Minister of China: We have noticed unrest in our western provinces particularly among the Uighur people. These border the central Asian Muslim populations. Although our government can control some of these outbreaks, tensions are on the rise and some of their partisans are planning uprisings. Our army is in position to terminate any of their plans. We have less tolerance than some of you in the West.

M.S.PLATT   THE LAST SUPPER

Prime Minister Britain: Our secret service agents can share some thoughts with you. Here is what we know. Our MI6 intelligence branch has learned that the bombing in Tel Aviv was a botched sabotage event. A terrorist group, probably from Iran, planned to destroy the Leviathan gas field operation. The explosion extended into the deeper caverns of the gas fields and caused the tsunami. The attacks in Iran are not fully explained yet. We are working on this. It is possible that the Saudis wanted to negate the Iranian nuclear plans before Iran had a bomb. The Iranians did not have 'clean hands' in our treaty negotiations and the Saudis found that out.

Prime Minister Russia: As long as these oil-producing countries gain wealth from their oil enterprises, the threat of terrorism will continue. My staff reviewed the terror activities over the last 30 years. It parallels the rise in income from oil profits in the Middle East countries. Saudi Arabia was an insignificant agricultural kingdom until oil was discovered there in the 1930's. The price of oil per barrel then was a meager $3 or less per barrel. The price rose to $16 to $20 in the 1950's. When the OPEC cartel organized in the early 1970's, the price of oil rose to $110 per barrel, and Arab hostility increased during the 1970's and 1980's.

PM/China: In 1971 the U.S. went off the gold standard. Suddenly, there was no measure of exchange in the market. The American dollar was used instead. But it was not the American dollar that became the standard. It was the rising price of a barrel of black-gold oil, and only the Middle East nations and their financiers benefited from the inflation that ensued. Wealth increased but at the expense of the nations that needed to buy oil.

PM/France: Even now Saudi Arabia has 18% of the petroleum reserves, and these will probably last for 90 more years. The Saudis are the largest exporters of oil and the second largest producers after Russia. They rely on oil for 88% of their revenues, and these may reach $224 billion in some years. Some of you in this room are the prime importers of this oil. The U.S. imports 14.3% of Saudi oil. China 13.7%. Japan 13.7%.

President/United States: Yes. We realize that the U.S. imports a lot of oil. Twenty-four percent of the petroleum consumed by the U.S. is imported. In 2015, we imported 9.4 million barrels of oil per day, and 16%

came from the Persian Gulf countries, 31% from the OPEC cartel. We, in the U.S. have responded by producing more oil—from offshore and shale sources. We account for about 9% of the world production of oil now. We are also buying more oil from Canada, about 40% of our imports, I believe.

PM/Russia: True. But consider. The Saudis produce 13% of the world production. Iraq, Iran and Kuwait produce 4% each. Our Russia accounts for 13% of the production.

PM/Britain: And the Saudis manipulate the market. Even now when there is an oil glut and markedly lower prices for oil, they are flooding the market and forcing U.S. shale oil companies to close their wells, even go out of business. If the Iran treaty continues, Iran will flood the market too. The Persian Gulf nations can afford to do this. It only costs the Saudis and Kuwait about $10 per barrel to produce oil. A lot of Saudi oil is near the surface and is under higher pressure so development and production costs are less. Our wells in the North Sea are more difficult to develop. It costs us about $50 a barrel.

M.S.PLATT   THE LAST SUPPER

President/United States: And our shale producers cannot make a profit unless oil commands $36 or more per barrel.

PM/China: Manufacturing in China has recently been reduced.   The government even lowered the value of the yuan and decreased purchases. Yet the oil glut continues.

PM/France: But the Saudis will continue to flood the market. They can produce at lower costs. They can borrow money on the open market. It is said that they could borrow $65 billion per year from 2015 to 2020, and that would only be 43% of their GDP.

PM/China: So applying market factors to limit income of these Persian Gulf nations may not work. If Iran began to flood the market after sanctions are lifted, these countries will only get richer. Iran already exports $95 billion in oil annually. It sends us in China 29% of their exports. And Iran still has 10% of the world's proven oil reserves and 15% of the gas reserves.

PM/Britain: Does not seem like an easy way to reduce the incomes of these nations. We just want to reduce their capacity to earn vast profits that permit them to create mischief and tyranny. If any of these countries obtain the funds and knowledge to buy or build nuclear weapons, international chaos will ensue. We will all be at the mercy of these Islamic nations. And Western culture, as we know it, will be defeated. Isn't that what fundamentalist Islam has wanted for 1400 years?

PM/China: May I make a suggestion? I don't think it would be wise to cause these Islamic nations to go bankrupt, or to cause economic chaos. This may be viewed worldwide as a form of genocide. After all, China needs some of the products that these nations produce. And we want to sell our products to them. But we want to prevent a nuclear holocaust.

President/United States: We five nations were the first to produce nuclear weapons, and we have a vast amount of weapon stockpiles. We are the only countries that agreed to a Non-Proliferation of Nuclear Weapons Treaty. Three other nations, possibly four, have not agreed to this treaty: Pakistan, India, North Korea, perhaps Israel. It is time that we flexed our muscles.

PM/France: How do you suggest we proceed?

PM/Russia: Ten countries produce 64% of the world oil. We produce 13%, China 5%, the U.S. 9%. That is almost 30%. And the U.S., China, Japan, India and Russia consume 40% of the world's production. We should have more leverage in these matters.

PM/China: We should form a cartel similar to the OPEC nations, and we should negotiate production and prices. We should also develop reciprocal trade agreements that would be to our advantage. I believe Japan and India would be interested in working with us. It would be to their advantage.

President/United States: What would that do to the nuclear threat?

PM/Russia: If this sphere of economic influence works together, we would trade most of the oil among ourselves. The Persian Gulf nations would not have a ready market for their goods. They could sell to whomever they wished, but not to us, and the supply/demand ratio would change. Suddenly, they would not be able to manipulate the market or make enormous profits. Ergo. No money to support terrorist mischief. And one thing more—those nations that do not sign a non-proliferation treaty should have their nuclear ambitions severely limited.

PM/Britain: How would you accomplish that?

PM/Russia: The economic sanctions would do that. The non-cooperating nations would lack the funds to compete in the world market. They would not be able to produce nuclear weapons. In time, they would be forced to work out a nuclear treaty.

President/United States: Somehow I am concerned. Aren't these economic sanctions that you are describing immoral?

PM/France: Isn't atomic war immoral? The Arab nations have been at war with us for 1400 years. And now, they threaten us with nuclear annihilation. Let Islam decide if it really wants to follow the teachings of Muhammad and seek brotherly love. After all, He clearly spelled it out in the Qur'an.

PM/China: And another thing. Let the Islamic nations decide if they want to enter the age of enlightenment. It is their decision. That is the moral thing to do.

PM/Britain: And maybe the West should consider re-entering the age of enlightenment. After all, the war and destruction that we have rendered in the past 200 years have not been one of enlightenment.

President/United States: I agree. Perhaps we should also revisit that area. We haven't done so well in our greed have we?

PM/Britain: But that approach still doesn't settle the Israeli-Palestine problem. It needs to be addressed.

PM/Russia: Well, the U.S. will need to press the Israelis to recognize Palestine as a nation. The Arabs will need to recognize Israel as a legitimate nation in the Middle East. They may resist, but economic sanctions by we five nations and the United Nations should prompt all the parties to agree to a resolution that has been festering for over 70 years. Jerusalem should be an International City, and freedom of religion should exist both in Israel and Palestine.

President/United States: You are more optimistic than I, but I believe the time has come to pursue this thing, or else we may find ourselves nuclear dust.

CHAPTER XIV

It was as if a miracle had taken place and as far as Kristin was concerned, the Messiah had returned and saved the world. Maybe some of the sinners inhabiting the earth were unworthy of His Grace, but saving the planet was indeed what happened. When challenged with the fact that none of us, even the righteous, had seen the Messiah, Kristin responded that since nuclear warfare had been abrogated, that was fact enough. Then she volunteered that any "Doubting Thomas" should have realized that. She would then press us further. It was now obvious that the Covenant with God was renewed. The pact with Israel had been restated, and a new Israel was now situated in the Holy Land. Not only with the Jews, but also with the people who now inhabit it whether they be Jews, Christians, Muslims, Buddhists, Hindu, or any other sect. According to Kristin, it was a matter of Faith. Had I not realized that? If one could not perform the 613 Commandments of the Jews, the Two of Jesus would do. God had chosen to share His love with those in the world who loved Him and who would love their fellow humans…their neighbors. He had told us that two thousand years ago when asked, "which is the great Commandment in the law?" And He said, "Thou shalt love the Lord, thy God, with all thy heart, and with all thy soul, and with all thy mind. This is the

M.S.PLATT   THE LAST SUPPER

First and Great Commandment. And a Second is like unto it. Thou shalt love thy neighbor as thyself. On these Two Commandments hang all the law and the prophets."

And then I realized, that in His love there was no room for murder, ...or stealing, or cheating, or lying. There was no need to envy my neighbors or commit adultery with them or to adulterate anything in the world. I did not need or want to be greedy for wealth or material things. I realized that the sin of mankind is to love the power of wealth and dominion of man over man. The savings grace of man is to love God and one's fellow neighbor. In fact, I should delight in sharing some of the things that God had given me.

Although the Darwinists had proclaimed in the mid-1850's that "only the fit survive in this harsh world", it would take two world wars and a threat of nuclear oblivion for us to realize that only God's love prevails. His creation is His gift to us, and we have the responsibility to be the stewards of this gift. In the cosmos of His world, He had given us many forms of energy. Oil... black gold, is not the only one. There is the sun, the winds, hydroelectric power, and the seas as well as the fossil fuels to harness.

And so, as the months did pass, I could see Neville Boy grow in the image of his father whom I knew and loved so well. I survived my "chimeric state" because of the goodness of dear friends, and I could feel my strength return.

Late one day, when the afternoon sun began to dip into the western waters of the Mediterranean, and its rays glittered the eastern Judean desert and Jerusalem, I remembered a time, not so long ago, when Neville and I first traveled to this perplexing land. And I remembered Neville searching the Jerusalem landscape, wondering what our visit would bring. Little did we know then what it would bring? But on this day, I looked at Kristin as the sun's luminous beams washed her face, and I was grateful for whatever this land did bring us.

At times, Kristin would tell me that she was happy being in a new land… in a new life…a new beginning… sharing her love with Neville Boy and me. And when Kristin and I would disagree, we would look for areas where we could agree. And when she found out that I did something nice for her and Neville Boy, she would

M.S.PLATT   THE LAST SUPPER

look at me with those luminescent blue-green eyes and with a little twist of surprise on her lips; and give me a gentile Christian hug and a tender kiss. And I knew...I knew... that she was happy. And I was happy within my heart...within my soul, made whole again.

M.S.PLATT   THE LAST SUPPER

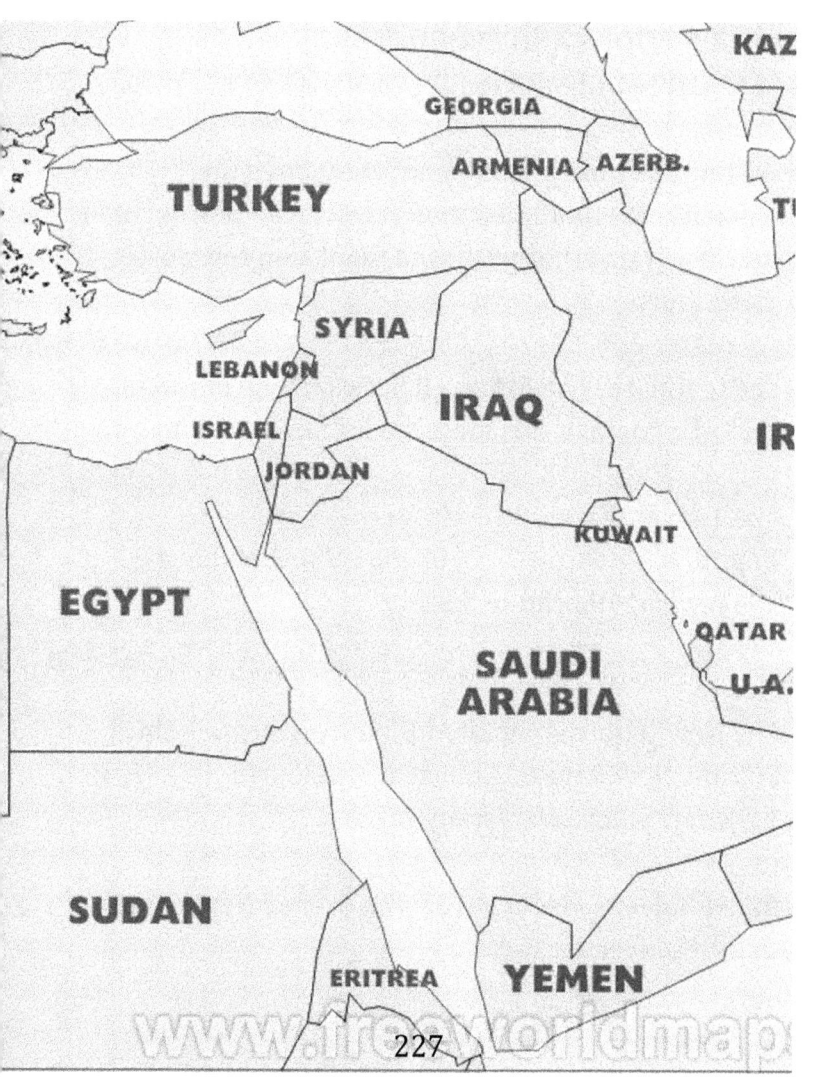

M.S.PLATT   THE LAST SUPPER

ATTRIBUTIONS AND PRODUCTION
ACKNOWLEDGEMENTS:

Writing a historical fiction novel requires the acquisition of multiple items of information from many sources. The author wishes to thank and recognize these sources:

The Chumash. The Art scroll Series/Stone Edition. (1993). Brooklyn, NY: Mesarah Publications, Ltd

The Tanakh. The Holy Scriptures According to Traditional Hebrew Text. (1985). Philadelphia, PA. The Jewish Publication Society

The New Oxford Annotated Bible, Augmented Third Edition, New Revised Standard Version. (2007). New York, NY. Oxford University Press

Abdel Haleem, MAS. (2010). *The Qur'an.* New York, NY. Oxford University Press

M.S.PLATT   THE LAST SUPPER

Patai, R. (2007). *The Arab Mind.* Tuscon, AZ
    Recovery Resources Press
Patai, R. (2007). *The Jewish Mind.* Long Island City, NY.
Hatherleigh Press

Attribution is also given for selected data obtained from
    https://en.wikipedia.org/wiki/ on topics dealing with:
Susa.
Kingdom_of_Israel (Samaria).
Kings_of_Judah.
Medes, Babylonia_captivity, Partha.
Neve_Tzedek.
Passover, Passover_Seder. Religious_relations_in_Israel.
Israel-United_States_relations.
Parthian_Empire.
Sasanian Empire.
Safavid_dynasty.
Early_Muslim_conquests.
Ottoman-Safavid_relations.
Israeli-Palestine_conflict: 1920_Nebi_Musa_riots.
Tsunami_bomb, Richter_magnitude_scale.
Leviathan_gas_field.

M.S.PLATT   THE LAST SUPPER

Human_leucocyte_antigens.
Chromosomes.
The Nuremberg_Laws.
The Economy_of_Iran.
SNP_genotype_sequencing.
Whole_genome_sequencing.
Single_nucleotide_polymorphism.
Genetic_studies_of_Jewish_origins.
The Age_of_Enlightenment.
Treblinka_extermination_camp.
Religion_in_Saudi_Arabia.
The Economy_of_Saudi_Arabia.
Bathyscaphe.
Nereus_(underwater_vehicle).

Numerous Internet blood bank resources.

Behar,DM. (2010). *The genome-wide structure of the Jewish people.* http://www.nature.com/journal/v466/n7303/abs/nature09103.html

Hirsh, M. (2004). *Bernard Lewis Revisited.*
http://www.washingtonmonthly.com/features/
041.html

Current Situation in Israel. (n.d.).
http://Middleeast.about.com/od/Israel/tp/
  Current Situations-in-Israel.htm

Numerous Internet sources from Google.com

Simple political map of the Middle East.
www.freeworldmaps.net/middleeast/

Edited by Anna Marie Barnum.

OTHER PUBLICATIONS BY THE AUTHOR:

"Do Not Forsake Me," Martin Luther King, Jr.—The Uncertainty of His American Dream. (2007 and 2012).

Holy Economics: Resolving the Debt Crisis. (2011).

Minyan: Ten Stories. (2008).

A Simplified Tax Structure for The United States. (2015).

The Myth: "Soak The Rich". (2015).

These are available from Amazon. com

M.S.PLATT   THE LAST SUPPER

M.S.PLATT   THE LAST SUPPER

www.ingramcontent.com/pod-product-compliance
Lightning Source LLC
Chambersburg PA
CBHW071451040426
42444CB00008B/1295